"As enchanting as it is fascinating: Andreas Viestad has a calm gift for evocative scene-setting, story-telling and, crucially, for making and exploring connections that bring everything illuminatingly to life." —*Nigella Lawson*

"Andreas Viestad has written a fascinating, thought-provoking and funny book about the importance of food in history. He zips seamlessly between the smells and flavors of a meal in a restaurant in Rome and the long lines of history." —*Alice Waters*

"A fascinating look at food and its history through the prism of one classic restaurant in Rome. Andreas Viestad has created a 'culinary archaeology' that's as erudite as it is gripping. He's as comfortable with amusing asides and anecdotes as he is with the deepest digs. His writing leaves you entranced, hugely enlightened—and hungry." —*Marina O'Loughlin*

"A uniquely beautiful, historical account of Andreas' two-hour meal at a well-known trattoria in the Campo dei Fiori area of Rome. For me, Rome is the eternal city and one that I love for its history, art, architecture, and food. Andreas has brought the history of the world to life through a meal at a Roman table. He writes an entertaining and beautifully written account of how food shapes not only who we are but where we were and where we go as humans. This is a wonderful addition to my collection of cookbooks and culinary memoirs and travel books. It is a book that tells the history of the world according to the food that is eaten on a leisurely afternoon in one of the world's most beautiful and historical cities.

A r

—*Lidia Bastianich*, author, cl

T0243166

"Insightful and enchanting. Viestad reminds us of the power of food and how it has greatly impacted the formation of world history." —*Eric Ripert*

"History and food memories are everlasting. They bring an eternal pleasure of time and place throughout the decades and centuries. This book reminds us of how deeply rooted food is in our travels, stories, and traditions." —*Daniel Boulud*

"If 'Culinary Archaeology' had been a course major back when I was in college, I just might have graduated with honors. Andreas Viestad takes us on an evocative journey through time, effortlessly weaving past and present, and transforming one classic Roman meal into an appetite-inducing learning experience. This is the best possible *insalata mista*: with equal parts cookbook, history lesson, travelogue, and fantasy. It's right up there with sitting in the Campo dei Fiori on a gorgeous spring day, devouring a hillock of crispy *carciofi alla guidea*." —*Danny Meyer*, restaurateur, author of *Setting the Table: The Transforming Power of Hospitality in Business*

"Everyone's dream is to visit Rome, to sit down at a restaurant and enjoy one Italian meal that makes you experience flavor, tradition, and passion all at the same time. Andreas Viestad's must-read *Dinner in Rome* takes things a step further, inviting you to travel with your mind and your palate. His two-hour dinner is a journey to last a lifetime." —*Cristina Bowerman*, chef patron, Glass Hostaria, Rome

"Fantastic book! Essential reading for anyone who loves Italian food and wants to immerse themselves in the incredible food culture of Italy." —*Giorgio Locatelli*, chef

DINNER
IN
ROME

A HISTORY OF THE
WORLD IN ONE MEAL

ANDREAS VIESTAD

Translated by Matt Bagguley

REAKTION BOOKS

Published by
REAKTION BOOKS LTD
Unit 32, Waterside
44–48 Wharf Road
London N1 7UX, UK

www.reaktionbooks.co.uk

First published in English 2022
First published in paperback 2023
English-language translation © Reaktion Books 2022
This book was first published in Norwegian in 2020 by Kagge Forlag AS
under the title *En middag i Roma: Verdenshistorien i et måltid*

Copyright © Andreas Viestad
First published by Kagge Forlag, 2020
Published in agreement with Oslo Literary Agency
Matt Bagguley asserts his moral right to be identified
as the translator of the work.

Printed and bound in Great Britain
by Clays Ltd, Elcograf S.p.A.

A catalogue record for this book is available from the British Library

ISBN 978 1 78914 782 7

CONTENTS

THE CENTER
OF THE UNIVERSE

L A CARBONARA is perhaps the best restaurant in Rome. It has too many guests, is too hectic, and has too high a turnover. It's in too prominent a location, quite simply. Yet I always end up here, after a long day of walking the cobblestones around the ruins, palaces, and museums of the Eternal City. The restaurant is located to the north of Campo de' Fiori, a busy square in the middle of Rome's historic center.

In the morning, the vegetable traders arrive in small trucks or overladen three-wheeled scooters. Then come the florists and those manning the tourist stalls that sell cured meats, truffle oil, and alphabet-shaped pasta. All day the place is crowded with people, a mix of Romans and tourists alike. Right now, as evening approaches, the bars along all sides of the square are filling up. The vendors are starting to pack away, leaving the area strewn with broken carnations and trampled cauliflower leaves. A small mechanical street cleaner, just slightly more effective than a regular broom, drives awkwardly between the stalls.

James Joyce once wrote disdainfully, "Rome reminds me of a man who lives by exhibiting to travelers his grandmother's corpse." And it is easy to see his point. History is everywhere. You can sit on the same marble steps the emperors sat on, walk on cobblestones that once ran with the blood of saints and gladiators, visit monuments to the madness and creativity of mankind, and see places that have been crucial to the development of Western civilization.

On my first visit to Rome, I wandered round with my eyes ablaze. If I wanted to walk from one part of the city to experience the sights in another, I would always stumble upon several other historic monuments on the way. It was fascinating, but also exhausting.

Things didn't get much better when I married an archeologist. For a profession where you live off studying, not people's grand-mothers, but their great-great-great-great-great-grandmothers' corpses or remains, Rome is the place. By experiencing the city through my wife's eyes, I learned to listen to Rome's history as told through its buildings and ruins. When she shows me around, we might stop at a cobblestone, an uneven surface, or a fragment of an ancient pillar in a far newer house. She has shown me how Rome is built upon ancient foundations, using materials from the city's many previous lives, and that even dilapidated buildings and ruins have a dignity of their own.

An ever-recurring subject among the archeologists I hang out with is fieldwork. These months or years of working on an excavation, digging and analyzing, continue to provide them with perspective and stimulation long after they—as most people do— end up behind a desk in a public office. Fieldwork gives them a lasting sense of feeling special, because they have, after all, experi-enced the jubilant triumph of being as close to history as you can get. "You're standing right where the previous inhabitants stood, with exactly the same object in your hands," my wife explains, radiating the same enthusiasm she tries to convey to her students.

History can speak to us through art, buildings, cobblestones, ruins, and simply through being present in a city that contains so much of the past. Luckily, once you feel saturated to the point of bursting, you can disengage from history with good food and drink, long evenings of mindless, worry-free enjoyment. Finally free! From the yoke of the past, from the never-ending history class! For a passing moment at table, with a bowl of pasta and a glass of wine, even James Joyce might enjoy himself and admit that Rome is a lovely place to be.

But it isn't correct to say that food is a passing thing, present and ephemeral, while marble and cobblestones are permanent, the only things with the ability to tell stories about the past. I am convinced that history is also present, maybe to an even greater degree, in the food we eat.

My fieldwork has been at the table. I have shaped my inner self—and my outer self—with more than 50,000 meals. I have eaten food, I have read about food, I have traveled to find out more about food and I have cooked. I have been lucky, smart, or cunning enough to turn my all-consuming interest in food into a profession.

The artifacts studied by archeologists are to a large extent hard: stones and bones, weapons, jewelry, metals, and money. Most of the historical sources concern matters that were deemed important enough to be written about, such as gold, generals, victories, and conquests. Food has the potential to tell another story: about where we come from, how we used to live, and what motivated and inspired us. Where an archeologist will use a posthole or the remains of a foundation to shed light on the past, I will use grains of salt, a bowl of pasta, and a glass of wine. Let me call it—even if for no other reason than to annoy my wife—culinary archeology.

Standing roughly in the middle of Campo de' Fiori is the statue of Giordano Bruno. Tour guides normally stop here to tell the story about the Dominican monk, mathematician, and astrologer whose work extended the Copernican Revolution. Like Copernicus, Bruno claimed that the stars were not things drawn on the firmament to give us something to look at. They were suns, like our own, just far, far away. He also claimed that the universe had no center, and that the world was ruled by the forces of nature. A bold theory, since it by extension meant that God was not all-powerful, the stories in the Bible not facts, and that the words of the papal church were not infallible. It went down about as well as you might expect: Bruno was arrested, convicted, and eventually burned at Campo de' Fiori on February 17, 1600. To prevent him from contaminating those present with his dangerous opinions, he had a metal plate attached to his tongue before he was led to the execution site. When a group of intellectuals, led by, among others, Walt Whitman, Victor Hugo, and Henrik Ibsen, erected the statue of Bruno in the square in 1889, there was fierce opposition from the Church. A threat even circulated that the pope would leave Rome should the city be disgraced by a statue of the heretical monk. Since then, the Campo de' Fiori has served as a place for anti-Church demonstrators to assemble. Look and you can sometimes spot where the authorities have removed graffiti saying, "A basso il Papa!"—down with the pope—from the nearby walls.

An old-fashioned account of the past, one I sometimes encountered when I studied history at university—and which is still prevalent in guidebooks and in many works about classical history—presents history as the sum of the actions and decisions of great men, a long list of generals and emperors. A more up-to-date understanding puts emphasis on material conditions, deep power structures, ideas, ideology, and property. What's hardly ever mentioned is the food, other than in relation to events that led to a famine or crisis, or the discovery of new resources. But food is not just a result of history. Sometimes food, I would argue, quite often in fact, is a driving force—sometimes *the* driving force—that made us settle in the places we did and organize ourselves how we did, that made us who we are today. But, as Giordano Bruno so heretically urged us, we have to change perspective in order to see it.

This book is about a dinner at a restaurant in Rome one evening in June, and what this meal—and every other meal—can tell us about our past. It is about the tastes that changed us, the ingredients that tamed us, the food that fed an empire, and the search for the origin of the world's greatest dish. In that respect I would say—not to put too fine a point on it—that there is more history in every lamb chop or bowl of pasta than in the Colosseum or any other building or historic monument. And unlike the buildings and cobblestones, the food we eat is as glorious and new every time, no matter how long a history it has.

A busker sings on the south side of Campo de' Fiori, competing with the music from the nearby bar. The smell of fried food and espresso merges with cigarette smoke as the last rays of today's sunlight flicker across the square. For a brief moment, the combination of sunlight and bird muck on Giordano Bruno's statue make it look like he has a glowing halo.

Such irony! As a result of his scientific work, Bruno was excommunicated by the pope and even banned by the Protestants in Germany. His books were placed on the *Index librorum prohibitorum*, the Catholic Church's list of banned books, where they remained until 1966. History has been harsh on Bruno's judges—with good reason—including the executioners who tied him to the stake with his head down and legs up, then set fire to him and let him burn. Today, most of his claims are widely accepted: they are now a part of our collective worldview. But he was wrong about one thing: on this mild June evening, it is quite obvious that the universe *does* have a center, and it is here, at Rome's Campo de' Fiori.

BREAD

I have barely sat down when the bread arrives at my table. The waiter, Angelo, hurries past on his way to the diners outside, and with an almost imperceptible hand gesture lands the bread basket in the middle of my table. In many restaurants in Italy you have to pay a cover charge for bread, called "coperto," which is normally about two euros per person. It's a practice hated by restaurant guests, who interpret it as a message saying, "We conned you," and in Rome it is now forbidden to demand coperto. But whether you have to pay or not, the bread you are served will often be totally bland, sometimes wrapped in plastic, as lifeless as cardboard.

This cannot be said of the coperto-free bread at La Carbonara. It is light and fluffy, with a crispy crust and a slight doughiness that gives it just the right amount of resistance when you chew. It is baked in the building next door, at Forno Campo de' Fiori, one of the few artisan bakeries to have survived the invasion of the large industrial bakeries that now dominate Italy. The apartment I am staying at is located in the block next door, with a terrace overlooking the square itself. I like to stand there in the morning watching the passers-by. When you observe the square from above, you notice how the flow of people suddenly changes when the bakery opens at 7.30 a.m., like a new tributary entering a pond or a lake.

Forno Campo de' Fiori is always full. What they offer changes throughout the day, from cornetti and cookies and pizza alla Romana (thin pizza-base-like breads with mortadella) in the morning, to the 3-foot-long pizza al taglio, more elaborate types of sweet pastries, and several different breads when they reopen in the afternoon.

The customers are, as they always are in Centro Storico, a mix of Romans and tourists. But although the tourists are surely a considerable and presumably desired—yes, even an *essential*—part of the bakery's clientele, it is as though they don't exist. Everything is done in Italian. And not only that: virtually all of the bakery's first-time customers have trouble coping with its intricate system for ordering and paying. Yet nobody attempts to simplify or explain. Every floundering new customer is met with utter impatience, as though they are the first one ever to have any difficulty. Order there, pay here, collect your order somewhere else. Everyone knows that! No need to explain or hang signs. I have lost count of how often I've been the idiot holding up the queue, since I always forget that in a bar you have to pay first and then collect the espresso, while in a bakery you have to order first, then pay, and then collect your order by showing your receipt.

This reluctance to become part of a globalized English-speaking community, where shopping is easy, where you can buy a coffee with milk after noon, and where shops don't suddenly close for several hours in the middle of the day, is a constant source of frustration for the foreigners I know who have settled in Rome, and for many Italians too. At the same time, it helps give the city its distinctive character. There is something attractive about this proud defiance, particularly when you don't have to live with it every day. It feels pretty humiliating when you're standing there, red-faced, after being told off in front of the rest of the congregation for your lack of Roman bakery customer etiquette. But once you have learned the system, you feel like a master. Now when I'm buying my cornetto, I'll look scornfully at the foreign first-time shopper doing everything wrong. If she looks friendly and bewildered, I'll help her. But if she is arrogant and demanding, I'll stand quietly with the other initiates in the queue, like a Roman among Romans.

Bread is an integral part of the meal in Rome for the same reasons it is elsewhere: it is a universal part of our food culture. A few years ago I was working in Zimbabwe, where they eat sadza, a glutinous maize porridge. It is regarded as their staple food, a main source of nutrition, and they eat it every day, often several times. After a while I got pretty tired of constantly eating sadza, so I took a packed lunch instead. "What's the staple food where you come from?" asked one of my colleagues, both fascinated and horrified that there was a place on the other side of the world where people didn't love eating sadza.

"We don't have a main food like you," I replied, before telling them about everything we eat back home in my native country, Norway: cod, salmon, lamb, cabbage, pork, and game such as elk and reindeer. Lots of different things depending on what season it is, or what we like and prefer. Another colleague burst out laughing.

"You're kidding! You eat bread for breakfast, as a snack, for lunch, as a side dish for dinner *and* for supper? You're addicted! See what's in front of you, man!"

I looked down at my sandwich and immediately realized that he was right.

I have eaten bread every day, my entire life. On a normal day I'll eat bread several times a day, for breakfast and lunch, sometimes in between meals. It often feels boring, and I constantly think I should be eating something more exciting. But it is bread that keeps me going. It has been this way for generations. And, for over 2,000 years, here in Rome.

Bread is the mandatory accompaniment in a restaurant—it can take the edge off the worst hunger, or help mop up the remaining pasta sauce or meat juice. At a nearby table, one of a group of young friends has ordered grilled sea bass, the restaurant's most expensive dish, while the others in the group have settled for simple pasta dishes. The tradition when eating out is to pay the Roman way, *pagare alla romana*, which involves splitting the bill equally without calculating precisely who has eaten what. They are presumably all well aware that they are paying for their friend's exclusive taste. One after the other, they dip their bread in the medley of stock, oil, and lemon juice on the fish's serving plate. If they are going to pay for it, they are at least going to taste it.

BREAD AND GRAIN have played a central role in Rome's history. Grain existed as a food, but also as a prerequisite for the city's growth, the growth of the entire Roman Empire, in fact. According to legend, the history of Rome starts with the arrival of a small group of people on the west coast of what is today Italy. "I sing of arms," writes the poet Virgil at the start of the Roman Empire's national poem *The Aeneid*,

> and the man, he who, exiled by fate, first came from the coast of Troy to Italy, and to Lavinian shores—hurled about endlessly by land and sea, by the will of the gods, by cruel Juno's remorseless anger, long suffering also in war, until he founded a city and brought his gods to Latium: from that the Latin people came, the lords of Alba Longa, the walls of noble Rome.

The story begins with the king's son Aeneas and his entourage settling in the area, which at the time was untamed and uncivilized. The landscape was covered by forest, and the people living here knew nothing about agriculture or farming. According to Virgil they had evolved from oak trees.

The city itself was founded a few generations later when two of Aeneas' descendants, the twin brothers Romulus and Remus, arrived on the scene. They had a complicated family history and were the result of their mother being raped by the god of war, Mars. As infants, the brothers were ordered to be killed by a jealous uncle but were rescued by a she-wolf and a woodpecker. The wolf suckled the boys. Exactly what the woodpecker helped with is less clear. That part of the story is often left out. As the two brothers grew up and set about founding the city, they began arguing about where it should be located: on the Palatine Hill, as Romulus wanted, or on the Aventine Hill, which Remus preferred. The quarrel ended with Romulus killing his brother and naming the new city after himself—in all modesty.

Romulus is said to have founded the city on the feast day of the shepherd-god Pales, April 21, 753 BC—and although people stopped taking the myth literally a long time ago, this date is the one most commonly used when calculating the age of the city. The two infants suckling the wolf is still Rome's symbol; the motif is visible everywhere. On the wall outside La Carbonara hang the remains of a poster for the football club AS Roma, whose logo is the wolf mother and the two children.

So the Romans are not—as most of the neighboring peoples are—the descendants of primitive indigenous people and oak trees. Instead they are the progeny of Aeneas of Troy. There is divine blood in their veins. And the city is founded on fratricide.

WHAT WE KNOW about the city's earliest history is based on myths, so most of it probably never took place. However, in the absence of other sources one has to rely on these fairy tales, perhaps hoping they are an expression of some deeper truth. If it did not happen exactly like this and with these exact participants, something similar could have happened, and probably did. The Roman historian Titus Livius, who was active at the start of the Common Era, admitted that there was probably more charm and poetry than there was truth in this part of the city's official history, yet he argues for it to be used nevertheless: "It is the privilege of antiquity to mingle divine things with human; it adds dignity to the past and if any nation deserves the right to a divine origin, it is our own."

What must have initially been a rather shabby collection of warriors, ruling over some impoverished shepherds on a small settlement on and around the Palatine Hill, gradually expanded into a considerable city-state, and then a regional power. Rome was brutal and militaristic, and, as a result of its aggression, very successful. Between the years 300 and 200 BC, the entire Italian peninsula was conquered and came under Rome's control. In the following centuries, this expansion continued at high speed into regions that eventually became referred to as the provinces— *provinciae*—and included the islands of Corsica, Sardinia, Sicily and the Balearic islands, the Iberian peninsula, the area that is now France and Belgium, the southern part of the British Isles, the Balkans, Greece, several parts of Asia Minor, and the Mediterranean coast of Africa. Rome wasn't built in a day, as the mythology and more recent, fact-based history can confirm. Two brothers became one, and then the greedy empire grew, house by house, man by man, village by village, province by province, country by country—until the Roman Empire comprised as many as 50 million inhabitants. By around 100 BC, there were already a million people living in Rome.

VIRGIL SINGS ABOUT arms and a man, and that is how most stories about the Roman Empire go. There are generals, statesmen, mad emperors, the occasional woman—preferably a temptress—philosophers, and traitors. There are intrigues, invasions, battles, and stories about an empire that became so huge it eventually covered almost the entire known world.

But what did they all live on? What did they eat? Something almost totally absent from the classic stories about Rome, and most of the tour-guide depictions of history, is what many of today's historians believe was a precondition for the Roman Empire's remarkable expansion: the unique food system. Rome was not built by kings, senators, consuls, or generals. The city was, as Evan Fraser and Andrew Rimas write in their book *Empires of Food*, built on wheat. This doesn't mean that everything revolved around wheat. But it was wheat that fueled the social machinery, one of the important elements that made it all happen, not unlike the role oil played in the twentieth century.

To start with, Rome is situated in a peculiar location. Why did the mighty Roman Empire originate right here, 18 miles (29 km) from the sea, in the middle of an area that by nature is neither the richest nor the most productive? At first, when it was still only one of many moderately successful cities, Rome was held back by its location. The Romans may have been more distinguished than their neighbors—after all, the family tree does include Trojan kings and gods—but they were poorer in terms of natural resources. Anyone who has traveled around Italy will have seen how fertile many other parts of the country are: the lushness of Tuscany and the Po valley, evergreen Umbria, and the vast fields of southern Italy and Sicily. These areas could feed large populations. Rome, on the other hand, had a limited amount of farmland and a population that was expanding rapidly and all the time. To feed the rising number of inhabitants, they quickly became dependent on grain imports. As a result, they built an advanced trading system. And that made all the difference. The statesman and philosopher Cicero believed that it was the city's location, and the fact that it was so dependent on trade, that laid the foundation for its later success:

Such a river enables the city to use the sea both for importing what it lacks and for exporting what it produces in superfluity; and by means of it likewise the city can not only bring in by sea but also obtain from the land, carried on its waters, whatever is most essential for its life and civilization. Consequently, it seems to me that Romulus must at the very beginning have had a divine intimation that the city would one day be the seat and hearthstone of a mighty empire.

Rome was always involved in some war or other with its neighbors. War and conflict were the norm at that time, and with each triumph it was the victor's right to plunder whatever he wanted. The rule had previously been to leave the battlefield and those defeated after inflicting a sufficient degree of humiliation upon them and collecting a reasonable dividend. In some special cases, such as when Rome finally defeated its archenemy Carthage after more than a hundred years of war, they would take everything they could, raze the city to the ground, and then sprinkle the ground with salt. Total annihilation. But they were exceptions. Normally it was enough for the enemy to have been defeated and weakened for one to go home feeling richer and stronger. What set Rome apart from previous major powers was that, where other victors returned home with the spoils, the Romans would remain in the conquered lands. Former adversaries were included in the continuously expanding state, and as they adapted they gradually gained more rights. Rome's influence could be brutal, but it was also possible to see the benefit, as in the Monty Python classic *Life of Brian*, where Reg the separatist leader rhetorically asks: "What have the Romans ever done for us?" His allies take the question literally and start listing everything from aqueducts and better medicine to sanitation, the legal system, education, better wine, and peace.

As the Roman Empire matured, an outstanding bureaucratic system developed that reached further and further into the provinces, with administrations and positions which were no longer dependent on individuals, families, and clans, where everyone was replaceable. After previously governing by a principle of alliance— where the defeated became allies, and, provided they remained loyal, were largely allowed to do as they wished—the new Roman state was now assimilating. The elites of the conquered provinces eventually began writing and speaking Latin, embracing Roman values, living in Roman houses, bathing in Roman baths, adopting Roman customs, and gaining civil liberties.

The Romans were able to govern a continuously expanding empire. And they had a reason for remaining in the conquered areas: the empire was largely built on its ability to collect taxes in the form of grain, olive oil, metal, or whatever the conquered areas had to offer. Where the conditions were right, new areas were cultivated so that more tax could be collected. This was in many ways the very dynamic of empire building. The grain provided rations for its army, which would maintain order in the provinces and in turn subjugate new areas. This enabled further expansion, which led to more income in the form of grain, and on it went. The largest empire the world had ever seen continued to swell like a rising sourdough, growing bigger and greedier the more it was fed.

Just as modern-day capitalism depends on economic growth—a positive feedback effect where money begets money: growth in one sector leads to growth in another, which leads to growth in another, and so on—the Roman Empire was dependent on pumping more and more grain into the system. As the author and journalist H. E. Jacob writes, wheat "was the mortar of life; which held the nation together." The Roman system was rich with silver and gold, since there was no shortage of looting and taxation—and Romans were in no way picky about how to collect its riches. But this growth was first and foremost made possible by grain.

When the Romans conquered areas that produced very little grain, they embarked upon large-scale tilling operations and simply transformed the regions into fields. When they reached England, the Romans found forests, crofts, and scrubland, but that all quickly came to an end; they drained the swamps and multiplied the production of grain. And for a long time England was the most important source of grain in the northern part of the empire. Scotland was left alone, perhaps not because of the fierceness of its resistance, as Scots like to think, but because the potential for producing grain there was far more limited.

The transportation of grain across vast bodies of water required a tremendous logistics operation—thousands of ships sailed constantly across the seas from the north and the south. It might sound laborious, but consider the alternative: While one ship was able move many tens of tonnes of grain, and eventually up to several hundred, by ox it's impossible to haul more than 250 pounds (115 kg) over any distance. You might cover 12 miles (19 km) per day at best, and 11 pounds (5 kg) of your load would have to be used as fodder, so before you got very far a large part of your cargo would have been eaten up.

The Romans had a near-perfect system, while it worked: extensive, safe, and secure, with an army that was generally well fed and content, and a capital where the impoverished hordes remained calm, as long as there was enough to eat. But the food supply was always its most vulnerable point. This became clear in the year 68 BC when an attack on the coastal city of Ostia threw the empire into a crisis. Much of the Roman fleet was destroyed by pirates who—when you think about it—were perhaps no more pirates than the Romans when they were out conquering and pillaging. Ostia was sacked and what couldn't be stolen was set alight, as were the grain reserves. The food for hundreds of thousands of Romans, which was stored in enormous warehouses near the port, went up in flames. In just a few days the price of grain had multiplied. The supply lines from outside were broken; the fleet was sunk. Strong, powerful Rome was immediately helpless. "Panic struck the city population as people realized that, trapped in an urban network of brick and marble, they might starve," write Fraser and Rimas.

The British writer and journalist Robert Harris compares the raid on Ostia to the attacks on the Twin Towers on September 11, 2001: "The perpetrators of this spectacular assault were not in the pay of any foreign power: no nation would have dared to attack Rome so provocatively." The pirates were outcasts, loosely organized terrorists capable of spreading fear far beyond what their true strength indicated. Who they were remains unclear. Some claim that the attack itself wasn't particularly unusual or dramatic, although it was used as an excuse to implement the measures that followed. The attack on Ostia had significant consequences internally. Just as the 9/11 attacks led to a broadening of authority for the police, military, and state intelligence—the scope of which tested the limits of the modern constitutional state and the principle of power sharing—the attack on Ostia led to a concentration of power that laid the foundations for the end of the Roman republic and the eventual fall of the empire that followed.

Before the pirate attack on Ostia, the Roman republic had been governed by a complicated power-sharing principle designed to hinder the development of a permanent dictatorship or a return to monarchic rule. During crises it was normal to appoint a leader with extended authority. The position, which was actually called *dictator*, was subject to a time limit and only gave authority to the individual in the area he had been assigned to straighten out. One of the worst things a politician could be accused of was to have ambitions of being king.

Although the principles of power sharing were often interrupted and the boundaries overstepped, they had, until then, been robust enough to prevent all power from being amassed by one person or family. The consuls who governed were appointed in pairs, often picked from rival groups to keep each other in check. Command of the military was assigned for limited periods and with a clearly restricted mandate. On several occasions the system had malfunctioned and had been on the verge of collapse. After the pirate attack on Ostia it was set aside—for good, as it turned out. The popular general Pompey the Great succeeded, with the help of various straw men, to pass an emergency law: *Lex Gabinia de piratis persequendis*—Gabinius' law concerning the pursuit (and punishing) of pirates. The law gave Pompey almost limitless power and a matching budget.

It didn't take him long to chase the pirates to the eastern corner of the Mediterranean, to what is now Turkey, where, after a brief siege, they were defeated and "exterminated." Upon Pompey's return he was celebrated with the full honors of the empire. Order had been reinstated, so it seemed. But it hadn't, of course; it had been turned on its head. In the years that followed Pompey was in charge, along with his two partners, Marcus Licinius Crassus and Julius Caesar. Where there had previously been a Senate, which had supreme power and authority, the empire was now ruled by a triumvirate consisting of three generals. The state no longer had control of the army: it was now the army that controlled the state.

Pompey was the most powerful general of the three, and when the pre-existing frictions between them became openly hostile it was presumed that he would come out on top. As we know, history would have it another way. Crassus got himself killed in battle fighting the Parthians during a failed attempt to subjugate new regions to the empire. His head was subsequently used as a prop in Parthian theater performances. Pompey was assassinated in Egypt, and he too was decapitated. It was Caesar who managed to keep his head attached to his body and eventually harvest the fruits of this slow-motion coup d'état.

After this, rule by emperors—perpetual tyranny, dictatorships under another name—was a fact. Concerns about what would happen if the food supplies were threatened and the impoverished masses revolted had led the ruling elite to swap the fine-tuned but vulnerable equilibrium of the republic for the security of a dictatorship. They believed it would only be a temporary measure, but it turned out to be the bane of the republic—and Caesar's too, incidentally. In the year 44 BC—after being in power for less than five years—Julius Caesar was killed. During a Senate meeting at the Theater of Pompey, the dictator was stabbed to death before the statue of his former ally and rival. The restaurant Da Pancrazio, which lies in an extension of Campo de' Fiori, its cellar a part of the Theater of Pompey, advertises that you can "eat where Caesar died."

Grain was absolutely essential, because not only was it a commodity and ration for the army but it also kept the peace, both out in the provinces and not least within the city itself. To have a million people collected in a city with such extreme disparities between rich and poor—and where the majority are poor—is a recipe for a powder keg. The city's rulers lived in constant and well-founded fear of rioting and public unrest, but a surplus of grain from the provinces offered them a powerful defense against rebellion: distribution of free, or heavily subsidized, grain rations to the poor masses. From the year 123 BC until the fall of the empire, grain rations were provided to all of Rome's inhabitants. "Bread and circuses" were essential for keeping the underclasses content. Much has been made of the public spectacles of gladiators and lions but bread was the more important.

The food supply was always the empire's soft underbelly, its Achilles heel, and the fear of revolt never stopped. In an article with the revealing title "A Starving Mob Has No Respect," the historian Paul Erdkamp writes about five hundred years of food riots in the Roman world. The emperors Tiberius and Claudius both experienced attacks by mobs when there were shortages of food. Sometimes, a mere rumor of a food shortage would be enough to cause trouble. In the year 190 BC, the military leader and Commodus' second-in-command Marcus Aurelius Cleander was blamed for rising food prices, and the raging mobs would not be satisfied until his decapitated head was put on display.

To secure the supply of food the grain trade came under the authority of the *prefectus annonae*, a powerful state-run office that served as both Ministry of Food and Department of Homeland Security. A system involving more than three hundred different food depots was established to insure them against hard times or attacks on facilities such as Ostia. The bakeries also began to be regulated, because even when there wasn't a food shortage, there was always a risk of civil unrest if the bakers were suspected of hiking their prices or selling bread that were smaller than the prescribed size. Under the control of the *prefectus annonae* the bakeries could almost be considered government employees, and this gave them a steady income, although they were furious about losing the chance to make a fantastic profit.

"Alexander the Great had traveled to Egypt to declare himself 'the son of the sun,'" wrote H. E. Jacob in *Six Thousand Years of Bread*. "But Caesar and Antony felt no such twinges of glory when they ascended the Nile. They wanted nothing but grain." Egypt was the empire's most important granary, and so crucial to its well-being and stability that it wasn't made into a normal province. It came under the emperor's direct control—his personal property, in practice. He couldn't risk some obstinate general or governor using Egypt's grain as leverage over Rome. He instead used the grain to boost his popularity with the masses. "Thus was established a profitable relationship between the billionaire emperor, the greatest landowner in the empire, and the Roman unemployed, the poor man of the capital," writes Jacob. "Egypt was the magic wand that linked Caesar to the proletariat, and the proletariat to Caesar. One gave bread, the other fists."

I RELAX WITH a glass of wine and do some people-watching. From my days as a restaurant critic, I've kept my old habit of arriving a few minutes earlier than the given time, instead of a few minutes later, as most guests seem to prefer. When a dinner starts at eight, I'll be there at five to. It means avoiding the bottleneck at the entrance, and having a better chance of winding my way to a different table if I'm offered one tucked out of sight or the slightly unattractive one by the toilet—and not least because it allows me to get a drink and a little bread, so that I don't crash from hunger.

When I arrived, La Carbonara was no more than half full. Now the ground floor is almost full. Most of the seating is on the first floor, which makes it possible to fill a restaurant that seems only big enough for twenty people with three, four, or even five times as many guests. There's a continuous stream of people going up the stairs. New arrivals, who don't have reservations, are told there's nothing available. They respond by pointing at the few tables that are empty, only to be told that they are reserved. The waiting staff run in and out carrying menus, wine lists, water, and wine.

I've always liked the fragile minutes when a restaurant is running beyond its capacity, when far too many guests are pouring in, hungry and full of expectation. Those who have been here a while already have to get their main course, new arrivals have to place their initial orders, and additional orders have to be made. This is the big restaurant test: can you up the tempo, work twice as hard, run fast without stressing, and still come across as graceful, friendly, and in control while squeezing through the crowds of hungry and sometimes unruly guests?

Much has been written about the Roman Empire's fall nearly five hundred years after Caeser. How could such a huge and powerful empire simply fall apart? It's easy to point at the threats from its external enemies, from the Huns, the Germans, and other barbarian peoples who by then were more organized and had picked up a lot of smart fighting tips, many of them from working as Roman mercenaries. You may have heard the hypothesis about how Rome's rulers became weak and insane from the lead used in the city's advanced plumbing system. Another quite widespread explanation concerned the Roman elite's decadence and detachment from reality. The Roman Empire was well known for its licentious extravagance, inbreeding and ostentatious consumption that could only be viewed as a sign that the end was near. Prokopios, the East Roman sixth-century historian, tells a story, perhaps not entirely true but illustrative anyway, about how Emperor Honorius reacted upon hearing that Rome had fallen after being sacked and humbled in the year 410:

> And he cried out and said, "And yet it has just eaten from my hands!" For he had a very large cock, Rome by name; and the eunuch [who had come with the message] comprehending his words said that it was the city of Rome which had perished at the hands of Alaric, and the emperor with a sigh of relief answered quickly: "But I thought that my fowl Rome had perished." So great, they say, was the folly with which this emperor was possessed.

Much of the criticism about Rome's rulers is correct. By our standards—well, by most standards—they were ineffective and foolish, and placed a huge emphasis on the consumption of luxury at the expense of almost everything else. At the same time, this explanation is perhaps just as much about moral condemnation, about how it seems right for the Romans to be punished for their gluttony and excess. In reality, the fall of the Roman Empire was more likely the result of death by a thousand cuts.

Or a thousand cuts and the blow of a dagger. The invading masses were bad, but not always much worse than what they replaced. After all, the empire had been at more or less constant war with its external enemies, and had usually found ways of crushing, bribing, or deterring them. The eccentricity of the elites was shocking at times, but you can't really claim that Honorius was any more detached from reality than, say, Caligula, who had made his horse a senator nearly four hundred years earlier. The Roman upper class had long been overly preoccupied with intrigues, power struggles, incest, the preparation of exotic foods and other eccentricities. The decadence of the elites certainly didn't make it easier to defend the empire, but although there was no shortage of delusional hedonists in the capital, it was a different story in the army.

Fraser and Rimas claim that the problem, with the Roman system of tax paid in the form of grain, was that the land in the provinces ended up being depleted. "Under the empire, arable land suffocated. It was farmed too greedily, and the loss of nutrients turned it barren." They also stress that there's no single explanation, but they do point to the connection between the rise and fall of the empire and what they call the rise and fall of the "food empire." In many places, the soil simply couldn't take any more. It was forced to yield too much, and as a result the harvests got smaller. Taxes were increased for those able to pay, which put even more pressure on the remaining agricultural areas, until the system finally broke down. Large areas of what was once Rome's granary—the provinces of North Africa—are now desert. According to Fraser and Rimas, the wheat that had helped create Rome's greatness also contributed to its downfall.

Far from everyone agrees with this portrayal of the collapse of soil quality and harvests. But when you look at the other factors that may have contributed to the empire's fall, several of them have also had consequences for the food system. Climate change—yes, they struggled with that back then too—meant that some of the more peripheral areas no longer produced as much food. On a political level the division of the Roman Empire into east and west meant that Rome no longer had access to Egypt's granaries. Rome was now diminished, and Constantinople took over as the new center.

BREAD IS FOOD. Bread is power. But it is also a symbol. "The farmer puts grain into the ground, as if burying the dead, and it is reborn as a plant which itself bears grain," writes the author Maguelonne Toussaint-Samat. Two nights ago I visited Sant' Andrea della Valle. The basilica is located three blocks northeast of Campo de' Fiori at the spot where a twelfth-century woman rescued the body of St. Sebastian from the sewer, into which he had been thrown after his death. This church is for some inexplicable reason dedicated not to Sebastian but to two Andrews: St. Andrew, "the first called" by Jesus' disciples, the patron saint of rope makers, butchers, and pregnant women, and protector against sore throats; and St. Andrew Avellina, the patron saint of Sicily and of stroke victims. From the street, it doesn't look particularly splendid: gray marble in between more gray marble. But it is truly magnificent inside, with all the art and seventeenth-century ornaments money could buy, including a relief of Jesus descending to limbo, a depressing motif with very little grounding in the Bible, and an equally unpleasant painting of Sebastian's corpse being hauled up from the sewer.

I stood there, alone in the church, wondering if I could detect the early signs of a sore throat or a stroke, when I noticed a piece of Communion bread lying on a narrow ledge by the crypt of St. Fortunatus. I've always been fascinated by the idea of Holy Communion—and especially the Catholic, almost cannibalistic notion that bread not only symbolizes but actually becomes the body of Jesus. However, as a nonbeliever with a degree of basic respect for other people's beliefs, I've never gone so far as taking Communion simply in order to satisfy my curiosity about the taste of the bread.

Now, on the other hand, with the wafer lying there right in front of me, I had an opportunity to taste it without having to deal with priest or congregation; there were no witnesses, apart from the deity and saints in which I didn't believe, and I didn't think they would mind, should they exist. To top it off, I was also quite peckish. It doesn't say anywhere what St. Fortunatus is the patron saint of, but I reckon it's probably misbehavior and snacking between meals. It turned out that the bread, which stuck to my tongue when I discreetly popped it into my mouth, wasn't actually bread at all. For the first few seconds it behaved a bit like a dry biscuit, sticking to my tongue, before it went limp and slippery and then dissolved completely. Had this been a restaurant, I would have sent it back.

If you're going to eat bread in church, does it have to be so boring? I wondered. Unfortunately, the short answer is yes, at least if you're a Catholic or Protestant. Mass-produced wafers have long been the norm, and several denominations have gone even further. In order to accommodate the increasing number of gluten-intolerant congregants, more and more congregations have switched to gluten-free wafers. These wafers are made not of wheat but of cornflour—from which the taste of corn has been removed. In other words, they're no longer bread, but mere symbols of bread.

In most places this is a change that has occurred without anybody protesting, seemingly because no one cares anymore.

But this hasn't always been the case. In the past, bread was a central theme, on a par with other matters of religious dogma. Theologians have disagreed not only about the meaning of bread but about the actual recipe for the body of Christ. By the eleventh century, very different ecclesiastical baking traditions had developed. In the east, they preferred to serve what Stewart Lee Allen, in his book *In the Devil's Garden*, calls "a well-risen, chewy Son of God": in other words, a bread much like a good sourdough. The Roman, western side preferred a dry, biscuity bread that hadn't risen, a forerunner to the machine-made wafer. Both sides believed that the other had misunderstood and served the wrong bread.

You might think that finding a compromise would be within reach: either the development of a common recipe, or simple acceptance that the bread varied slightly in different places. But such an each-to-his-own logic doesn't work when it comes to our Savior manifested as bread. Also, in the eleventh century the mood for cooperation within the Church was poor. The Church's best theologians tried to find a solution, but instead of reducing the disagreements as the work proceeded, the conflict escalated. The Roman Church viewed itself as superior to the eastern side; after all, the pope was a direct descendant of St. Peter. The Eastern Church, for its part, saw itself as the true center of the Christian world, since all the power was now in Constantinople. They looked down on Rome, which after six hundred years of decline had become a provincial city with a dubious reputation and a history that wasn't entirely glorious.

"Unleavened bread is dead and lifeless," wrote the Orthodox Patriarch of Constantinople, Michael Cerularius, to Pope Leo IX, "for it lacks leaven, which is the soul, and salt, which is the mind of the Messiah." On the Roman side, Cardinal Humbert had been appointed as the Western Church's expert on baked produce. Humbert was known as a fanatic with a difficult temperament and his response to the patriarch was in line with his reputation: "If you do not with stubborn mind stand in opposition to the plain truth, you will have to think as we do and admit that during meal [the Last Supper], it was unleavened bread Jesus Christ distributed." Had Humbert been a saint, he would most likely have been the patron saint of rebukes and reprimands.

The Roman tradition, which is quite clear in Cardinal Humbert's letter, is based on Jewish matzo—unleavened (or unfermented) bread—which Jews eat at Passover to commemorate their exodus from Egypt. Humbert is probably right about it being the bread Jesus ate. The Orthodox, however, were not trying to recreate the Last Supper but were more interested in the connection between the rising of the bread and the Resurrection. They also wanted to distance themselves from the religion's Jewish origins, and accused the Western Church of being "Judaists." At one point, Kerularius closed all of Constantinople's Roman churches and had his men storm in and trample all the communion bread they could find. That showed them!

To an infidel, it's almost incomprehensible that these two different pieces of bread—neither of them particularly tasty—held so much power. But it was this controversy over the bread, along with the Romans' inclusion of the word *filioque* ("and from the Son") in the text of the Creed, that triggered the Great Schism—the final division of the Catholic and the Orthodox Church.

"The first and most significant cause of the rift between them and us is the unleavened bread," wrote John VII, one of the leaders of the Greek Orthodox Church, as he weighed up the schism in the late twelfth century. "This theme contains the whole question of true faith in God. If it is not healed, the disease of the Church itself will not be healed."

I SIP MY wine and take small bites of bread while enjoying the controlled chaos of the restaurant. Freshly baked bread, when it's both soft and hard, is something I can never get enough of. Today's ordinary, secular bread is totally different to the bread peasants ate all over Europe, including my ancestors on their smallholdings in southern Norway. Their bread was coarse and hard, made from wholewheat flour. During lean years, of which there were plenty, they would also mix the grain with a non-wheat flour. Fishmeal was probably the most common for my relatives, but potatoes, seaweed, and bark were also used by other poor farmers. The bread itself was baked at home on the farm in simple ovens similar to the one beneath the old kitchen fireplace on my family farm, which dates back to the eighteenth century. You warm the oven section using wood or twigs until enough heat is stored in its walls for baking. It's a process that takes many hours, fills the entire kitchen with smoke, and doesn't exactly create optimal bread. This farmer's bread was mostly hard and flat. Baking was not something you could do every day, probably not even every week, so bread was often dried and sometimes hung up in the fireplace to prevent it getting moldy or eaten by mice. When it was eaten, hard pieces would be broken off, or more likely chopped off, then softened in a soup or broth.

Roman bread, however, must have been quite similar to what we eat today. It was made by professional bakers in large bakeries and, from literature, we know that the ancient Romans valued many of the same qualities in bread that we do. They also distinguished between bread's various degrees of coarseness. Barley was very tasty, but it didn't rise very well. Wheat was preferable, and the whiter it was, the better. At first, white bread was reserved for the richest people, but over time the expectation of having white bread spread to the whole population. One of our most important sources about everyday life in Roman times is the city of Pompeii; frozen in time by ash from the volcano Vesuvius, which erupted in the year AD 79, until it was excavated again in the nineteenth century. Excavations of the city show us exactly what the bakery and its bread looked like, and it hasn't changed all that much. The ancient Roman oven was a masterpiece of classical architecture. It may be 2,000 years old, but it makes my old oven, built nearly 1,800 years later, look just what it is—crude and primitive, something an isolated farmer on the world's periphery would use. The Roman version had a vaulted ceiling, its own ash drawer, a damper, and a water tank that enabled bakers to add moisture during the baking process in order to give the bread a nice, golden crust. The classic Roman bread was—and still is—round, and had four grooves, or a double cross if you will, so that it can be easily divided into eight equal pieces. In most places technology has changed profoundly during the two millennia that Pompeii's oven lay preserved under ash, but the oven used at Forno Campo de' Fiori remains almost unchanged since Roman times.

Unfortunately, out of pure distraction, I've eaten most of my bread. I curse myself. If I was steadfast about one thing as a res-taurant critic, it was to stay away from bread. Taste it, then leave it. Save room for what's to come.

ANTIPASTO

The filmmaker Federico Fellini claimed that it's easier to be faithful to a restaurant than to a woman. His claim, of course, says a lot about a certain generation of Italian men. But it also says something about the quality of classic restaurants, particularly Roman restaurants like La Carbonara. Nowadays most of the Western world is dominated by restaurants that seem desperately preoccupied with the present, modern restaurants that are perpetually obliged to offer the guest something new, and more often than not ending up like culinary opportunists and weather vanes. It's a trend which is inspired by the top restaurants, the true innovators. Noma in Copenhagen, for example, makes a living from reinventing itself. It has its own research department, who travel the world in search of inspiration and new and exotic ingredients; the whole menu is changed several times a year, and they never put the same dish on twice, no matter how good it is. Eating at Noma is a pleasure, of course, but that is not the most important quality of the meal. Its most valuable asset is that it is new. From this and other paragons of modernity the desire to change, to be innovative, has had a contagious effect. Keeping up, preferably at the front of the pack, is what matters. The modern restaurant is built around the chef and his (because it's nearly always a man) creativity and genius. If you eat there, you expect to experience something new; new ingredients, new techniques, and if the dishes are not completely novel—innovation, like all genuine creativity, is a rarity—there are new versions or interpretations. You go there to be surprised. To get something you couldn't get at home.

The classic Roman restaurant is different. It sells the idea of something that never changes—the feeling that you have come home when you walk through the door. La Carbonara has regulars who have been lunching or dining here almost every week for fifty years. As a casual visitor to Rome for roughly 25 years, I'm considered a newcomer.

People need restaurants, somewhere where they can take refuge, whether it's from life's hustle and bustle or other slightly bigger problems and challenges. A few years ago I was in Maputo, Mozambique. Just outside the city is Costa do Sol, a beachfront restaurant serving simple yet well-prepared Portuguese-Mozambican cuisine: grilled shrimp, grilled chicken, salads, and ice-cold watery beers. The country had recently lived through several decades of political chaos and civil war, and at one point the front line of the conflict was less than a mile from the city's beach. Nevertheless, the restaurant stayed open every single day.

IT'S NOT YET eight o'clock, but a thick blanket of dark cloud has gathered in the sky outside. The street vendors in Campo de' Fiori use this expedited dusk as an opportunity to get their evening sales off to an extra early start; since most of them are selling luminous objects of some sort, they need a degree of darkness. Rumor has it that many of them are illegal immigrants, organized by a criminal cartel that equips them with merchandise and controls most aspects of their lives. The items on offer vary, and whenever I'm in Rome the selection is a little different. It seems to go in waves, where one luminous gadget replaces another, but all the sellers will consistently offer the same thing. Last time I was here, they had small fireballs that flashed and put on a beautiful light show as they span round. This time it's a ball that flashes red and blue and for a few seconds hovers motionlessly in the air. If you have children with you—or if you just end up a little drunk in the evening, missing your kids at home—it's easy to be tempted to buy one. As I have done myself. It looked like one of the most amazing things I'd ever seen. As soon as I got home, it stopped working.

WHEN I BEGAN dining at La Carbonara, which must have been one of the first times I visited Rome, perhaps with a girlfriend at some point in the 1990s, the outdoor seating reached both corners and spread across nearly all of the 50 or 75 feet (15–23 m) down toward the fountain. There was a special atmosphere there, halfway out on the square. There were over a hundred chairs beneath oversized umbrellas, with rows of potted plants marking the perimeter. It was exactly how an outdoor restaurant should be. You were a separate group—an exclusive gathering who had white tablecloths, black-clad waiters, stemmed glasses, and wine coolers—yet you were still a part of the life on the square, with all the sounds, smells, and sales pressure it entails. The most persistent street vendors had a little trick: They would offer roses, in a slightly humble, pity-poor-me way initially. If that didn't work out, they switched to a more demanding, almost taunting, don't-you-love-your-girlfriend-anymore stance. And if the vendor felt like that wasn't working either, he'd open his hand and flash a bag of white powder and a lump of silver foil at you—that is, if you were young and considered within the target group.

In 2014, the authorities drastically reduced the amount of space La Carbonara was permitted to use for outdoor dining. Now there are only a dozen seats outside. Where you would have once felt like you were in the VIP area of a festival, waving hopefully for the waiter to notice you, it's now easy to feel a bit like a vulnerable minority; six small tables don't provide much of a counterweight to the hordes in the enormous square.

I nearly always eat inside, which is what most Italians do anyway. The restaurant's narrow, ground-floor room has undergone a facelift and I'm not quite sure if it's been entirely successful. The place has lost some of its worn old-world charm. Where there had once been wood paneling on the walls, there is now some kind of ruffled fabric. The chairs, which used to be the hard, uncomfortable sort made from reddish-brown wood, are today equally uncomfortable designer chairs in orchid purple, pale blue, aquamarine, grass green, and warm sienna. Like lipstick on the collar of someone you love, they arouse the suspicion that I missed something important while I was away. Fortunately, they have kept the old paintings hanging high up by the ceiling—generic, smoke-stained pictures of rural scenes that always remind me of an expression about how the art in restaurants is often as good as the food in museums: it's as it should be—better art would have outshone the experience.

FORTUNATELY, THE MOST important things about La Carbonara are the same as they have always been: the smells of roasted meat, steaming pasta, and expensive perfume that fill the rooms; the clinking of glass and the sound of voices. When the door opens the city intrudes, with the roar of the crowd in the piazza and the music from the nearby bars and the sound of the occasional moped or speeding car engine cutting through the air. Most importantly, the food is largely the same. The restaurant is owned by Maria

Trancassini and her husband Dario Martelli. Maria is the grand-daughter of the restaurant's founders. Dario once showed me a menu from 1961, pointing proudly at the dishes his wife's grand-mother used to make, most of which were still on the menu—one by one—until he came to the most important dish of all, the pasta car-bonara itself. He flicked the pages back and forth nervously, clearly stressed, like a priest realizing that part of the trinity is missing. "*Holy spiiirit!* Where are you?" Then he found it, not hidden away but printed in large letters, at the top of the menu. Pasta carbonara was the headliner sixty years ago.

Apparently, the staff are the same as they've always been too. The waiter Angelo has worked here for 45 years, nearly as long as I've lived. When I first ate here, he was already a veteran with thousands of evening shifts under his belt. His movements are quick and efficient, as always. Should you hesitate to order, he'll vanish, then appear like a genie when you put down your menu to indicate that you're ready.

I like his bony face and the sense that he's always been here. In a way, I also like the fact that he never recognizes me. Even when I've been eating at the restaurant for several days in a row, he'll still fail to show any hint of recognition. He'll always remember who ordered what, even when we are a large group, and set the plates with a steady hand, and pour wine into the strangely small wine glasses without spilling a drop. But he never looks at our faces, not mine, at least.

The job of recognizing people goes to Anne Luziette. It's hard to say what Anne's role in the restaurant actually is. Whenever I've asked what her position is she has always deftly avoided bestowing on herself a title. She doesn't call herself a restaurant manager or general manager or headwaiter. "A friend of the family," she says.

"And everybody else," she could add. Because while Angelo is cold and efficient, a man who wears his uniform unreservedly, Anne is the epitome of friendliness. Always discreetly dressed in an elegant suit. Always with a kind word for the regulars.

"Welcome, Dottore! Your usual table?"

"Nice to see you again, Signora Orsini, your sister is waiting for you on the first floor."

IN A WAY, restaurants as institutions are as old as civilization itself. Ever since we've had cities and trade, it's been necessary to have places where food can be served outside the home; anything from a seat at the table on a farm to a purpose-built eatery on a major thoroughfare. As the cities grew, so did the demand for more and more places serving food. Two thousand years ago Rome already had a million inhabitants; a trader, laborer, or craftsman working far from home needed food. It was more convenient to have it served there than to bring food along on the commute. In Pompeii and the neighboring city of Herculaneum—two places that offer us a snapshot of everyday Roman life—the remains of restaurants, which once provided food, drink, and, not least, an informal social arena, have been found. The excavations have revealed various examples of graffiti showing just how informal this arena was; some of them could almost be described as restaurant reviews, or perhaps more like early versions of the often highly subjective guest reviews on TripAdvisor: "Apelles and Dexter ate here most agreeably and had a screw at the same time," it says on the wall outside a combined restaurant and brothel in Herculaneum. "The food here is poison," reads a warning outside an establishment in Pompeii.

For the first thousand years or so, restaurants served food without the clientele having much say over what kind of food they got. It would be a pot of something boiling, a table, and sometimes, but not always, plates. For a long time it was normal for guests to bring their own cutlery. The restaurant as we know it emerged in France during the late eighteenth century and was a distinctly bourgeois institution in stark contrast to both the social life of the nobility, with its ritualized hierarchy, and the more raucous eateries of the kind where Apelles and Dexter indulged themselves in more ways than one.

At a restaurant or café people could gather as cultivated equals. It was a place where they could freely discuss what they wanted. And, equally new, it was a place where you could decide what you wanted to eat. Beef for me, halibut for you. Most restaurants offered a set of standard dishes but also allowed room for creativity, and the chefs would compete to be the best. After the French Revolution, many chefs who had previously worked for the nobility found themselves unemployed while the bourgeoisie simultaneously flourished. The number of restaurants therefore exploded, first in France and eventually throughout the rest of Europe and the major cities in the United States.

The father of gastronomy, Jean-Anthelme Brillat-Savarin, in his book *The Physiology of Taste* (1825), defined a restaurant as a place that allowed people to eat when they wanted, what they wanted, and how much they wanted, at a predefined price. It sounds so obvious, and nowadays it's easy to forget how revolutionary the classic restaurant was, and in a way still is. It is a place that exists for you; it stages a theater piece where you play the lead role and write the dialogue; it is somewhere you are looked after and where you get exactly what you want.

I BECAME INTERESTED in food just at the time when modern restaurants triumphed and everything had to be shiny and new. I relished it, living in the age of discovery, standing on the shore of a gastronomic ocean that constantly flooded me with new experiences. As mentioned earlier, I worked as a restaurant critic for a while, and later on the job partly involved writing about new restaurants and gastronomic trends. What's the brightest new star and how does it twinkle? What's the next big thing? What are the latest innovations?

I was so used to novelty that when I first encountered this classic restaurant, with its faded grandeur and never-changing signature dishes, in one of the most beautiful squares in the heart of an ancient city, it made a deep impression. I fell for La Carbonara and I've stayed faithful, in a way. It's my restaurant, I think to myself while sitting here. I stroke my fingers over the menu, caress it for a few seconds before opening it. Studying it closely, even though I know exactly what I want.

But of course, it's not always been La Carbonara. My first love in Rome was Il Drappo, a small family-run restaurant where Valentina Tolu, a gaunt-looking Sardinian woman in her sixties, worked the kitchen while her son managed the room while helping himself to the libations. The now shuttered restaurant was located in a tiny side street a few blocks northwest of Campo de' Fiori. I can't quite remember how I ended up there, but I remember my first meal and my first meeting with Valentina.

The place didn't have a regular à la carte menu so according to Brillat-Savarin it might not have been a proper restaurant; I was simply asked if I wanted meat or fish, and my response decided whether I got red or white wine in the carafe.

Then the food started coming. A modest celery salad to begin. Then *crema di pecorino*, a kind of cream cheese made from sheep's milk that was mild and soft and sharp all at once. There were cured meats, including mutton and boar from the Sardinian mountains; smoked swordfish, which came brushed with lemon and oil; and squid with orange and potatoes. I had my first encounter with *bottarga*, cured mullet roe that had a rich and pungently fishy taste, like a mixture of anchovies and soy sauce. Olives and artichokes were served drenched in olive oil. I'd never quite understood the point of artichokes before, but now I sat there undressing one, leaf after leaf, until I came to the heart.

When this culinary marathon was over, I sat back, replete and satisfied, only to discover that the meal wasn't over. Technically, it hadn't even begun.

"Antipasto" literally means "before the meal," and I can't be the only person to have been surprised and exhausted at the extent of this Italian culinary foreplay. I've often been almost unable to continue when the time came for the main course, or I should say the main *courses*. When Valentina came out with a huge portion of wild boar ragù and pasta, I realized that just being full wasn't going to be sufficient. And when she then served a whole rabbit, it was clear that I would be reaching the final stage of satiety: despair, when you can't manage to eat any more, but cannot give up either.

AS I WALKED around Campo de' Fiori earlier, I noticed how the vegetable stalls were piled up with artichokes. The first Roman artichokes from Civitavecchia arrive on the market in March, and are gradually followed by many other varieties: green ones the size of cabbage heads, beautiful purple ones, and prickly and thistly ones from Sardinia. The Romans are obsessed with what they call "artichoke season," referring to it as though it's just a small window of time, like for asparagus and truffles, but which in the case of artichokes seems to last for large parts of the year, from early spring to late autumn. I've come to understand that it marks the time when the temperature is comfortable in Rome, when you can drink coffee at the street cafés and enjoy being outside. When the weather's cold and miserable, the Romans will refuse to dress sensibly and instead go around shivering in their light, elegant jackets, waiting for artichoke season to come.

The artichoke can be a wonderful element in a pasta or a salad, or as an accompaniment to meat. But if you really want to enjoy this delightful thistle, there are only two options: *carciofi alla Romana*, which is a whole, boiled artichoke; or *carciofi alla giudia*, which is what I order.

The origin of *carciofi alla giudia*—"Jewish-style artichokes," as it's translated in old books—is completely unknown. No one is quite sure why it's associated with the Jews either, but today it's considered an important part of Italian cuisine, and one of the few parts of *la cucina ebraica-romanesca*—Roman-Jewish cooking—to have become a household dish. The recipe is evidently simple: fresh artichokes, trimmed and fried in oil.

When it arrives on my table at La Carbonara, I'm reminded of my first meal at Valentina's restaurant. What an impossible, strange ingredient, so loaded with frustrations, both in the kitchen and at the table. What little there is of an artichoke that's edible is wrapped in huge amounts of tough, fibrous thistle leaves. Trimming an artichoke is easy, on paper—"cut off the artichoke's hard outer layers and the bristles in the middle"—but this requires a special knife and a good cook. Once at Il Drappo, I got to join Valentina in the kitchen, where she gave me a few simple tasks like rinsing capers and sun-dried tomatoes, and picking the leaves of various herbs. Gradually I advanced to chopping rabbits into smaller pieces. But when I tried my hand at the artichokes, Valentina quickly said stop. One little mistake, and you might cut away most of the edible part. Go in too heavy-handed, or with a blunt knife, and you could lose a finger. My hands are a strange combination—office fingers, delicate and smooth, but with a number of little scars that look as if they could have been from some long-forgotten war. However, a not insignificant number of them are from when I grew artichokes and regularly came under small, unintentional attacks from myself.

At the table, the artichoke is nearly as difficult. Knives and forks are useless. Some people do try to use cutlery, but it's like eating a quail or any other small bird: the only thing that really works is to eat it with fingers, teeth, and patience, peeling off leaf after leaf and gnawing at the tiny soft pith, until you reach the core. With a pile of gnawed leaves accumulating on your plate, it can feel like you're only making very slow progress. Each bite is so tiny it simply increases your appetite. Then, just as you're about to give up, you come to what's called the heart, at the bottom, which is encircled by the very softest leaves. And I don't know of many other things that are better.

This whole process is where the expression *la politica del carciofo*—the politics of the artichoke—originates. The artichoke-eating technique was the House of Savoy's strategy for conquering and uniting Italy, piece by piece. The expression was coined in the eighteenth century by King Carlo Emmanuel III, when—with their eyes firmly on the target—they began claiming new regions. Some parts of the country were conquered by force; others were incorporated into the Savoy kingdom through marriage. Each piece seemed insignificant until the flesh-rich heart was finally reached. In the

1860s, all the leaves had been plucked, Italy had been collected, and then—in 1871—Rome was once again given the status of capital.

The Romans' love affair with the artichoke, and its even stranger relative the cardoon, or artichoke thistle—which is more or less the same plant, but doesn't have the head of an artichoke—dates back many thousands of years. What both vegetables have in common is how insanely bitter they are when raw—and uniquely sweet they are when cooked.

The taste comes in several waves. First comes the mild, discreet vegetable flavor and a consistency unlike anything else in the vegetable world. Then comes another wave that doesn't actually belong to the artichoke but incorporates a substance called cynarin, which affects the tongue's taste receptors and makes everything we eat and drink taste sweeter. What more could you ask of a thistle with a heart of gold? I take a sip of water, and it tastes sweet, almost like milk. The wine, which would normally have a rough edge from the tannins, now tastes smooth and fruity. I have seen the confusion that arises when someone—inadvertently or through an act of sabotage—serves artichoke at a wine tasting. Even the experienced wine tasters are suddenly unable to tell the difference between Burgundy and Brunello, or dry Chablis and sweet Riesling. Had you known no better, you might suspect you'd been spiked with some kind of taste hallucinogen. But if you know the secrets of the artichoke, and know that this is a short-term effect, you can savor a few minutes where the whole world is sweet.

OIL

The taste of the fried artichoke has two levels: one is the specific and unique taste of the artichoke itself and the shock of sweetness it brings; the other is a flavor that gives you an immediate sense of where you are in the world. It's a taste that crops up everywhere, and yet it's the basis of everything—from the simplest salad, to pasta, fish, and meat dishes: the taste of olive oil.

During my first stay at an Italian *agriturismo*—a combination of restaurant, hotel, and farm, complete with grapevines, chickens, some half-tame yet still quite scary wild boar, a rosemary bush, and an olive grove—I was surprised in the morning to be served a wonderful breakfast with eggs, freshly baked bread, and homemade jams but no sign of any butter. Granted, there was a small bottle of the house olive oil on the table, but was I really supposed to put oil on the bread?

"Look around," said my companion. "Do you see green valleys and cows grazing, or do you see parched hillsides and wizened olive trees? That's the main rule when eating in Italy: you eat what you see." It's perhaps taking the assumption too far, but there's no doubt a grain of truth in such romanticized statements. Here, in the metropolis of Rome, where there's all the international fast food, local junk, and trans fats a heart attack could wish for, it's the smell of olive oil you notice as you walk through the back streets, and the smell of fried food wafts out of the restaurant, and private, kitchen windows.

The artichoke is deep-fried in olive oil at a temperature some-where between 320 and 340°F (160–170°C). And as if boiling it in liters of oil wasn't enough, it is then served with fresh oil on the side, so you can dip the leaves in it once again. The boiling oil makes the vegetable crispy and hard, while the fresh oil gives the dish an extra dimension, a soft and fruity contrast to the thistle's crispy surface.

Olive oil is the most distinct characteristic of Mediterranean cuisine, and has been for over 3,000 years. The artichokes aren't just served with any old oil. The oil is fresh and grassy, a light green color, and it has an astringency that tickles the back of your palate ever so slightly. I start to eat and before long Anne comes over with a bottle that she proudly shows to me. She tells me that the fresh oil is extra-virgin oil from the farm of the Trancassini family, who own La Carbonara. The farm is located in Divino Amore—divine love—in the municipality of Marino. What was once a day's travel into the countryside, about 12 miles (19 km) from Campo de' Fiori, is now gradually about to be swallowed up by the expanding city's greedy appetite, with houses and apartments creeping closer every year. Just after the Second World War, nearly all the land in the area was owned by three farmers, one of whom was Maria Trancassini's father. While the mother ran the restaurant, the father took care of the farm. Now Maria's husband, Dario, is responsible for both. After his mother-in-law grew old and sick, Dario quit his job as a lawyer in the Vatican to take over the family business. He went from being the pope's employee to the pope's neighbor; the head of the Catholic Church's summer residence is located in Castelgandolfo, just a few miles from the farm in Divino Amore. When I asked him how the transition to working for the family business had been, he simply replied that his previous employer was a saint, which was actually true, in the literal sense, since Pope John Paul II was canonized in 2014. Could he also have been implying that he wouldn't use the same term for his mother-in-law?

Since the time of the Roman Empire, owning a farm in the country has been something all rich Roman citizens have craved. A yearning for the country that's been partly about having the option to escape the stifling summer heat in the city. In the very olden days, it was convenient to have somewhere to retreat to during plagues, sieges, or periods of civil unrest. It was also equally important to be able to do what Anne is now doing on behalf of the family: presenting the oil from the family farm, and preferably the wine as well. It shows, both literally and symbolically, that your roots run deep.

Rome is full of ruins. The city is a ragged patchwork of the past and present, where today's new developments and expansions try to exist between the occupying forces of the past. Ancient squares and protected columns can force new streets to suddenly become dangerously narrow for two-way traffic. At the Argentino bus stop in Corso Vittorio Emanuele II, you can look down into a deep hole showing the remains of Campus Martius, where hundreds of ownerless cats live among the ruins of the baths and temples. Beneath the ground, the city's drinking-water pipes thread their way up, down, and around to avoid damaging tombs, ancient temples, or any other ancient remains. Construction of the city's metro system is proceeding notoriously slowly because of the regularly occurring archeological finds. Much of Rome's visible history is the remains of important buildings of great historical significance. But far from all were monuments to greatness; good portions of them may have been curiosities in their time or historical parentheses. An emperor could demand that a memorial be built to celebrate his family, as Emperor Domitian did with the famous Arch of Titus at the Roman

Forum. Just over ten years later, Domitian was killed and condemned to "eternal oblivion" by the Senate. But the triumphal arch is still there, almost 2,000 years later.

Food is quite different. It may well be a necessity that we cannot do without, and is therefore more important than both palaces and places of worship, but unlike marble and cobblestones it is digestible. It comes out again after being used, and disappears into the sewer and into the ground. Eaten means eaten; it fills latrines but doesn't build monuments. One exception, however, is Rome's olive oil. Two miles south of Campo de' Fiori, right by the ancient city walls, is the former loading area of the ships that brought supplies up the river Tiber. Nearby is Monte Testaccio, which as mountains go isn't particularly impressive, standing 130 feet (40 m) high, covering an area of 5 acres (2 ha). But the mountain is not really a mountain; rather, it is a man-made structure rivaling the size of Rome's most majestic building, the Colosseum, a painstakingly constructed mound made entirely of amphorae—large clay pots. Testaccio is a huge spoil heap, a monument to the consumption of olive oil.

The clay pots, every single one, were used to transport olive oil to Rome's inhabitants. After being unloaded and emptied, they were broken up and meticulously stacked. Today, the mound is partly covered by trees and bushes, but it is still possible to see patches of layered pottery shards. In several places caves have been dug into the mound, some of which are used as garages and workshops, others as nightclubs and restaurants. The top of the mound is now closed to the public; it had previously served as a stand-in for the hill of Golgotha in Easter processions that reconstructed Jesus' final walk with the Cross. During the Middle Ages, it was used for pre-Lenten celebrations where carts loaded with barrels of live pigs would be rolled to the bottom, where the poor pigs would be instantly massacred and roasted, for the amusement of the spectators.

The oil's origin—which can be identified by the shape of and sometimes the markings on the various clay pots—was mostly Spain and the African provinces which are now Tunisia and Libya. Altogether, Monte Testaccio consists of over 50 million clay pots, which would have contained a total of 900 million gallons of olive oil. This enormous and beautiful scrap heap only represents the oil imported by the state; the oil distributed to soldiers and the poor through the *prefectus annonae*, the powerful Ministry of Food and Security. There were also private imports on a similar if not larger scale; only the richest and most distinguished families could boast of oil from their own farms.

Amphorae were the most-used freight containers of the age, and could contain a range of commodities, including grain and wine. There are various hypotheses about why only olive oil amphorae were used to make the structure at Testaccio. One explanation could be that after shipping the porous pots were partially saturated with oil. While the pots that previously contained grain or wine could be reused for anything, from flowerpots to the aggregate used for buildings and roads, the oil jars would eventually smell rancid; and if you mixed them with cement, which contained lime, the result would be more like soap—certainly not what you'd use for building a road.

Olive oil has nourished Rome's richest and poorest for millennia, and does so to this day. It is part of what Maguelonne Toussaint-Samat calls "the fundamental trinity," which consists of grain, oil, and wine. This is what Mediterranean food culture—and in many ways Mediterranean culture as a whole—is built on. "A good land," according to the Book of Deuteronomy, "is a land of wheat and barley, with vines, fig trees and pomegranates, a land of olive oil and honey." During antiquity, olive oil—along with grain— was about as important as the oil from the petroleum industry is today.

The first powerful cities on the Mediterranean coast were nearly all heavily involved in the olive oil trade. Just as it was with salt and wheat, the import and distribution of oil were subject to taxation and state control. This represented a sizable income for the Roman state, just as it had been for the Greek and Phoenician city-states previously.

When Noah sailed around in his floating zoo after the Great Flood, it was a bird with an olive branch in its beak that signaled that God's wrath had subsided; that they were near land and could start life anew. Olives differ from wheat and other agricultural commodities in that being an olive farmer requires a different perspective. The tree is a symbol of prosperity and peace—because that's exactly what it needs. After war and devastation, soil can be recultivated, but if olive trees get damaged they need a small eternity to grow back. It takes an olive tree ten years to go from a seedling to bearing fruit, and a generation or more before it will yield a decent crop. That's why they say you don't plant an olive tree for yourself, but for your children and grandchildren. However, once the tree has borne fruit it can live for a thousand years. It will just stand there and shower you with its gifts. The taste of olive oil was and still is the very foundation of the various Mediterranean cuisines, from Spain and Morocco in the west, to Lebanon, Israel, and Turkey in the east. But this oil has something else too, a symbolic, perhaps even spiritual, dimension that means it can hardly be reduced to just a type of fat, a source of flavor and calories. Let's, if only to simplify a little, call it a cultural dimension.

On the outskirts of Jerusalem lies Gethsemane, a garden at the foot of the Mount of Olives. While the rest of Jerusalem has been ravaged by countless religious wars, the olive grove opposite the Temple Mount looks much as it did 2,000 years ago. It's an area of reddish-brown soil full of crooked old olive trees with huge trunks and wispy growths of leaves at the top. I had read about these ancient trees, and when I was in Jerusalem a few years ago, I visited the Mount of Olives hoping to taste the oil. The olive grove belongs to the order of Franciscans, and I'd arranged to meet a Franciscan monk called Diego who lived in a little house in the middle of the Garden of Gethsemane. It was raining, so Diego welcomed me inside where a picture of Pope Francis hung on the wall, along with several photographs of volunteer groups working during previous olive harvests.

The monk showed me places where the olive grove is mentioned in the Bible: Luke, Mark, Matthew, John, and the Acts of the Apostles. According to the Bible, Gethsemane was where Jesus walked on the last night of his life. It was here that he prayed, so consumed by the fear of death that "his sweat became like drops of blood falling to the ground." And it was here that he was arrested after his betrayal by Judas. Regardless of what you believe in, this is one of those stories that has helped shape the world. It was later found out—or made up—that the Virgin Mary, conveniently enough, is also buried here. Diego had over the years developed a close relationship with the olive trees in the garden. To him they were more than old trees; he saw parallels between the hunched giants he'd been entrusted to look after and the religion he had dedicated his life to. "When a tree grows old, it doesn't have to die," he explained to me. You can take a cutting from an old tree, and, if it successfully germinates, a tree with the mother-tree's DNA will grow.

The oldest trees at the bottom of the garden are such offshoots. "It's possible that they originate from the time of Jesus," said Diego.

The idea of the trees dating from Jesus' time has long been part of the myth of Gethsemane. Today, the very oldest trees in the garden are fenced off, because, as with the pieces of the cross and other holy relics, this conviction has inspired pilgrims to steal twigs. Man's need for spirituality may be great, but there's obviously just as great a need for something tangible to bring home and brag about. However, contrary to the Legend of the True Cross, Gethsemane's oil story might be rooted in some truth. In recent years, Italian researchers have examined the trees in the garden. They have taken DNA samples, performed carbon dating, and found that all of the oldest trees, eight huge and impressively gnarled olive trees in the garden's lower section, are in fact the same tree. They are clones of a tree that stood there before them. Carbon dating shows that they are more than nine hundred years old.

Just how old the predecessor with the same DNA became, no one is certain. The Italian arborist Antonio Cimato from the Italian Institute of Tree and Timber, who led the dating work, claims that the trees in Gethsemane are some of the oldest olive trees in existence. He wonders whether they were propagated when the mother-tree was about to say its final farewell—in order to maintain the holy connection. For those who want to believe, the trees are proof of eternal life.

Diego found a loaf of bread and a bottle of oil, which he held up to the light before pouring it into a bowl. The oil was still a bit cloudy, as it often is for the first few months. I dipped my bread into it and watched it turn light green from the oil it absorbed. As I chewed it, the oil seeped back out, spicy and aromatic, fresh and fatty. When it comes to olive oil tasting, I've learned that you should compare the flavor of the oil with apple peel, freshly cut grass, and nuts, but the best way to describe the oil from the Garden of Gethsemane is to say that it tasted intensely like olive, to a far greater extent than anything I had tasted before. Like the oil at La Carbonara, and other good olive oils, this too had a peppery quality that made the back of your mouth tingle a little. It almost burns a little; it hurts, in a slightly pleasant way.

When the rain stopped, Diego and I went out into the garden, which was already full of people—pilgrims from all over the world on the journey of a lifetime. We stood there, with our hands full of bread and oil from the Mount of Olives, and before we knew what was happening we had a crowd of people around us. Without having planned it, we started dipping pieces of bread in the oil and handing it to the pilgrims. And a kind of wave ran through the congregation, as if they instinctively knew that something special was going on. "Holy oil from the holy garden!"

For a few minutes we were inundated by believers from the Philippines, Syria, the United States, Canada, France, Spain, and the Ivory Coast. Everyone wanted a taste of bread and the oil that was somewhat greater than themselves. And when the bread ran out, people dipped their fingers in the oil. One of them crossed themselves with it.

The oil, explained Diego, is not normally shared with the visitors. "Some of it is used in the household. The rest is sent to the Holy Father in Rome." In other words, the pope doesn't have to make do with the oil from his property in Castelgandolfo; he gets his from the trees Jesus walked among during his final days. I got to bring a bottle of oil home with me as well. There was something about it, something more than the taste. The certainty of it being special transformed the dining experience more than I'd expected.

A simple portion of fish or meat no longer needed sauce; a few drops of oil was all I needed to give it an exceptional flavor. When I found that someone had inadvertently used the oil to fry eggs, I was furious. It seemed like sacrilege.

Although the distinctions are more fluid these days, it's still possible to group different food cultures based on the type of fat they use. A modest vegetable or meat soup can be more or less the same in Italy or Germany or Norway: cheap meat and vegetables cooked for a long time. Yet the underlying flavor will be different, because in Italy it has the fresh breath of olive oil at its core, while we in the north would probably brown the meat in butter and serve it with bread and butter, not bread and oil. At the start of the common era, the Greek historian Strabo wrote about the curious folk of a faraway country who used butter as "their very own oil," while his Roman counterpart Pliny refers to butter as the food of barbarians.

In a way, he was right. The Vikings and a number of Celtic nations had a penchant for a type of fermented butter that was probably just as pungent as a funky cheese and contained such large amounts of oxidized fat that many of today's eaters would have considered it biohazardous material, not food. While many of the lard-eating peoples of Central Europe converted to butter during the Middle Ages, the oil-loving southern Europeans never got a taste for it. Toussaint-Samat writes about Catalan merchants who took oil with them on their travels through butter-eating regions. Butter was rumored to cause diseases, such as leprosy, so it was best to take precautions. The butter eaters, on the other hand, were equally skeptical about olive oil. Also, the quality of the oil that reached the northern countries was often so-so: the exported oil was usually the worst kind and would often go off, although not in a way that appealed to the connoisseurs of oxidized butter.

The food we eat helps distinguish between "us" and "them," between the barbaric and the civilized. So it has always been difficult to get those who have been used to eating butter to switch to oil, and vice versa. Toussaint-Samat also writes about the fifteenth-century king René of Anjou, who received several barrels of olive oil as a gift from his subjects when he moved to Provence. Unable to conceal his disgust when faced with the oil, he had cows brought in from his native Anjou in northern France so that he could have his fix of butter instead. Even now—when most of us are used to alternating between oil and butter, and don't have as much pride or identity connected to what kind of fat we eat for dinner—we can agree that a Béarnaise sauce made with olive oil, or an aioli using butter, does not taste right at all. Northern European and American fans of Mediterranean food will serve Italian food at dinner parties, but they'll have butter on their bread.

After the collapse of the empire, Rome too fell into decline. From the tenth century until well into the fifteenth, the city was little more than a shabby collection of formerly magnificent buildings. At its least populated, only 30,000 people lived in the city once inhabited by a million. Rome had little secular power, and the clergy were not always much to brag about either. In the first part of the fourteenth century, the Church was struck by the harrowing distress of the papacy moving to Avignon, the pope's so-called Babylonian Captivity. In the latter part of the century, there was open conflict between the pope in Rome and the pope in Avignon, both cheats and pretenders in each other's eyes. For a while there were three popes who all proclaimed their own virtuousness and excommunicated each other. When the Church finally managed to escape this civil-war-like predicament in the early fifteenth century and once again gathered in Rome, it was morally bankrupt.

It was also financially bankrupt. So to fill its coffers, the Church ramped up the sales of indulgences. Old religious rules and decrees were tightened and new ones made up to strengthen the Church's influence and income base. It was under these circumstances that butter first became affected by Church regulations. On fasting days it was forbidden to eat butter, or use lard, which was the second choice in most butter-eating regions. The butter ban applied during the forty-day fast, during Advent, on every Friday, and on the numerous public holidays and days commemorating saints—almost every other day was a fast, of one kind or another.

The papal decrees were expensive and impractical, and consequently unpopular—and there were a lot of them. The restrictions on butter were far from the only thing making everyday life complicated. You already had to pay the Church a tithe. And on the week's only day off you were required to attend long services, in Latin, where few—if any—understood what was being said. The Church had an opinion about whom you could sleep with, how you should sleep with them, and on what days you could do it. The priesthood had influence over "your coming and going both now and forevermore," as it states in the psalm, and—one might add— most of what took place in between. This is how the world often was at that time: full of unreasonable rules and decrees from above. The social contract—if you can call it that—implied that those who governed were expected to make life miserable for their subjects.

But one can go too far, and that's just what the pope of Rome did. The pope himself could enjoy the oil from his personal olive grove in Castelgandolfo or from the Mount of Olives in Jerusalem, and for most southern Europeans olive oil was the cheapest option. Not so for northern Europeans. If you lived in the green landscape of the far north, with grazing cows producing tasty milk from which you and all those around you could make delicious butter, it would feel exceedingly unreasonable when someone demanded that you spend a fortune on rancid oil from the parched expanses of the south. "They think that eating butter is a greater sin than lying, swearing or committing fornication," wrote a German butter lover and critic of the pope in 1520. "The people at Rome themselves scoff at fasts, and leave us in the provinces to use as food oil with which they would not grease their shoes. But they sell us permission to eat butter."

The butter-loving critic was a priest from Wittenberg named Martin Luther. Luther's criticism of the Church applied to a wide range of things and had both theological and moral aspects, but in butter he had found an issue that mattered to people and engaged them. The butter issue illustrated his overall criticism of the Papal Church almost perfectly: he claimed it was more interested in the ways it could obtain money than it was with right and wrong. The butter ban had no biblical foundation and was just a clever and vicious way to generate revenue. What people had on their bread couldn't possibly be God's main concern, he claimed.

The French historian Jean-Louis Flandrin has pointed out that the border between Protestant and Catholic countries today—with the exception of France—is almost identical to the border between butter-eating and oil-eating countries. For lay people, the conflict that led to the division of the Church was not about catechism and theology, but the freedom to eat the way they had always done.

SALT

Right in front of me on the table is a salt shaker, a little transparent jar of snow on a silver tray. When I think about it, it's most likely steel of some kind, shiny enough to be presentable but not valuable enough to be interesting to thieves or light-fingered guests. The salt shaker is such a natural detail that you barely notice it, despite there being one on every table in the room. There's no need to interrupt the conversation or look around for a waiter if you want to salt your food, since you can just reach out your hand automatically. It's the same wherever you are: salt is a matter of course at restaurants and on dinner tables in large parts of the world.

When the sweetness of the artichoke has subsided on my tongue, I stroke my finger discreetly over the perforated top of the salt shaker. I feel the tiny grains of salt against my fingertip. When I lick the salt from my finger, hopefully with equal discretion, I'm struck by the hard, metallic taste. I love the taste of salt.

Salt is ever present, even when it's not visibly in front of you. It is one of the fundamental ingredients of cooking. You need salt for baking bread, making soup, when you're going to fry a piece of meat or fish, when you cook pasta, or eat eggs—in short, most things. A kitchen without salt is possible, but only in theory. Imagine bread, soup, fish, meat, pasta, and eggs, and how any of these things taste without salt. And then, even worse: imagine everything, an entire diet, without salt. Unsalted bread with unsalted soup, unsalted fish with unsalted pasta. A life without salt would be a life of pallid, lackluster flavors. Food without salt just tastes less like itself. And to go even further than this initial, obvious declaration, I'll say this: a life without salt is a poorer life.

At home in the kitchen, I have built up a little salt collection. Over the years, it has grown to include between forty and fifty different types of salt from different parts of the world. During certain parts of my life I've traveled quite a lot, and eventually I saw no point in taking classic souvenirs home with me. There were strange-looking hats, jars and vases, coffee cups and carved figures, none of which even made it onto the mantelpiece or the pride of place in the guest toilet before they were sent to the loft, joining other souvenirs in cardboard boxes that were never to be opened. But I have always gotten something out of salt. My souvenir salts are reminders of places I have been, and how lucky I am to be able to make a living from traveling and eating, and writing about it, like the lucky winner of some kind of career lottery. And this salt—small bags and boxes from Réunion, Cape Verde, Peru, Mexico, Italy, and France—is something I use every single day.

The salt my son found on the rocks near Paternoster in South Africa, where the wild and cold Atlantic Ocean lashes the barren terrain under a merciless sun, looked like slush in an otherwise nondescript little puddle. It reminded me of ice about to crystalize, but instead of dissolving when I picked it up, the fine, white salt grains became hard in my hands as the excess water drained away. It eventually dried into porous lumps. Now, when I add it to boiling pasta water, the air trapped inside makes the tiny pockets between the salt crystals expand, and the lumps dissolve almost like magic. It sizzles for a moment and then the pot looks like it's about to boil over before the salt disappears.

Many of the other salts behave differently. My blocks of Himalayan salt are pink and compact and beautifully patterned, like the Valencia marble used in expensive hotel bathrooms. The rectangular slabs can be used for roasting: just heat them in the oven and put meat or fish on top. You would expect the result to be blisteringly salty, but at a high temperature the blocks act more like stones than salt. You might detect a saltiness on the fish skin or the outside of the meat, but otherwise it works just like a regular pizza stone. Afterward, when it has cooled down, you can rinse and dry the salt block, and it will be as good as new.

The volcanic salt from Hawaii is black as night, but when you grind it up, the food doesn't become dark and dramatic, as I'd hoped. At best—or worst—it just looks slightly dirty.

The obelisk-shaped block from the Wieliczka salt mine in Poland is a variety of pale, gray-white shades, and doesn't look terribly appealing, to be honest. But if you stand it on a light box or in the window and let the sun shine through it, it will sparkle as if there is someone inside playing with the light.

The most beautiful and exclusive crystals—those that form on top of the brine when it crystallizes—look like tiny pyramids, if you look closely. Each salt crystal is, like a snowflake, unique. And like snow, this uniqueness is not random; it appears in patterns, depending on where and, not least, how the salt is made. There is soft powdery salt, hard crusty salt, salt that resembles hailstones or tiny drops of sleet. The Maldon salt from the ancient Maldon saltworks in Essex in eastern England looks and tastes different to the salt from North Sea Salt Works on the west coast of Norway, or the salt from Noirmoutier in France—although all three are what the French refer to as *fleur de sel*, "flower of salt."

Looking at my trays of salt jars, and the bags and boxes of different specialty salts from all over the world, you can easily see that I've been affected by the soaring interest in salt recently. It's a foodie phenomenon with a touch of stupidity, and prices that are hard to defend. I'm embarrassed to admit it, but the block of Himalayan salt cost about $45, and even cheap salt can be expensive when acquired from remote locations. When I bought salt from the workers at the Marakkanam salt flats in Tamil Nadu, southern India, they couldn't understand what I meant when I asked for 2 pounds (1 kg). They stood there, on a mountain of coarse salt weighing hundreds of tons, shoveling it into huge sacks. The result was that, for the equivalent of barely a dollar, I left with a 50-pound (20 kg) sack which cost me a hundred times more than the purchase price in excess baggage on the flight home.

I'm constantly fascinated by just how different the salts in my collection are, to the degree that when I mention it to my guests, they're first impressed, then often perplexed. How should one react to all these salts? What's the right way to use them? And since people are often most concerned with themselves, it also tends to make them insecure: are they doing something wrong, since they don't have a whole selection of different salts?

I try to reassure them. Despite all its variations, salt is salt. Nearly all the salt we eat consists of somewhere between 98 and 100 percent sodium chloride. The only difference between the Himalayan salt and the coarse salt you buy in large sacks for $2—which can be used for salting both your pasta water and the front drive when it's icy and slippery—is that the Himalayan salt contains enough iron oxide to give the crystals a nice pink color.

The chemistry is the same. And in a way, so is the taste.

At a salt tasting during the 2001 International Workshop for Molecular Gastronomy in Erice, Sicily, described in Jeffrey Steingarten's book *It Must've Been Something I Ate*, the participants—mostly chefs and scientists—were invited to see if they could taste the difference between the famous salt from Ile de Ré in France, the local salt from Trapani, Japanese salt from Oshima, and regular table salt.

At first it wasn't difficult, since they are all quite distinct. The table salt, which is ground into small, evenly sized grains, tastes hard and metallic. The salt from Trapani reminds you of the sun-soaked Mediterranean, the salt from Ile de Ré of Atlantic sea spray, and the Japanese salt is known to be mild and creamy. But when the different salts were dissolved in water, it suddenly became impossible to distinguish them. Steingarten reported that only one of the participants was able to tell one from the other; "the identity of whom modesty prevents me from disclosing," he added.

I was there myself, and remember the spread of disbelief when the results were presented. Are all the different salts just a bluff? There were steely fronts, in general accordance with a split that often occurred at this workshop, namely between the scientists and chefs. Despite the modern and future-orientated tone of the whole gathering, the chefs mobilized to defend the ingredients they cherished and used daily, stubbornly claiming that the result would have been different had the tasting been done another way. Had the brine just been a bit stronger or a bit weaker, had the temperature been a bit higher or a bit lower, had the tasters just been different—me instead of him, perhaps? The result was surprising, yet gratifying to the scientists. It confirmed a basic scientific belief that salt, like everything else, is simply made up of atoms and molecules, and that chefs and gourmets are living in the Middle Ages, governed more by superstition and semi-religious beliefs than by knowledge. At first, in the 1990s and early 2000s—before the technology, the powder, and the foam took over—molecular gastronomy was about pointing a sharp, scientific light into the semi-darkness of the kitchen. It wasn't so much about inventing new dishes or using fancy new machinery to challenge tradition. Centuries-old home recipes would be subjected to empirical tests. Ingredients would be analyzed, and for many scientists there was an unspoken desire to "reveal" the various traditional products, a desire to show that the emperor, dressed in his *old* clothes, was naked.

I am neither a chef nor a scientist, so I wasn't quite sure what to think until, not long after the seminar, I had dinner at the home of Hervé This—the father of molecular gastronomy, and the man who had arranged the entire workshop. Also at the table was the head of research at L'Oréal, or one of the other big cosmetics firms, at least—I no longer remember. What I do remember, though, is that I asked this head of research if there really is any difference between cheap and expensive shampoos and moisturizers.

"What do you mean by *really*?" he said. "If by *'really a differ-ence'* you're asking whether you'll get dirtier hair or wrinklier from using the cheap products, there's no certainty that there's any dif-ference. What is certain, however, is that there's a difference in the experience of well-being," he replied. It's about everything, from external things such as the packaging, he explained, to the qualities of the product itself, like its fragrance and texture. These factors are undeniably at play, although they probably don't make much difference to hygiene or wrinkles.

And so it is with salt. When you taste the various types of salts, it's striking how different they all seem. Anyone with an interest in food, who has stopped and tasted a selection of different-looking salts, has also found that they taste different. Maldon salt *does* have other qualities than fine table salt, but they're not mainly—perhaps not at all—about what the salt contains or where it comes from. It's all about the salt's construction, about the texture.

Different types of salt will have crystallized in different ways, which means it will dissolve in different ways. Table salt, which is ground to a fine powder, dissolves almost immediately. One gram of salt ground to a fine powder can have a thousand times more surface area than a one-gram lump or flake of salt, and the fine salt can often taste hard and sharp because it dissolves so quickly on the tongue. Maldon salt and other *fleur de sel*, with its beautiful pyramid-shaped crystals, dissolves slowly and has a milder taste; sometimes it's almost as if there's an element of sweetness to it, mostly because of the way it dissolves. In addition, tiny mineral traces on the surface can help create subtle nuances in flavor.

When you use salt *in* your food, you cannot know which one you've used. As the salt-tasting in Sicily illustrated, it will have dissolved, and whatever minerals and other impurities it contained will have been evenly distributed. And unless the salt contains a high amount of impurities, or strong-tasting ones, like the Indian black salt that contains so much sulfur that it makes everything taste and smell of rotten eggs and deadly farts, you will probably not be able to taste the impurities. I know of people who insist that the taste is milder when they use Maldon salt or kosher salt in their soup or pasta water, and sharper when they use regular table salt. There are two possible explanations for this: one is that they're using the same volume of salt, and are therefore over-salting when they use fine table salt (tiny grains of salt pack more closely together, so there can be up to four times more salt in a teaspoon of fine salt than in a teaspoon of Maldon or kosher salt). The second reason is that the knowledge that you've used the very best ingredient will affect your perception of taste. The more you have invested in the food, the more you appreciate it.

It's only if you salt the food just before serving, like the sprinkle of *fleur de sel* on a piece of fish, or coarse salt on a steak—when you can feel the crystals dissolving on your tongue—that you notice the difference. Since being struck by this realization, I've been less afflicted by the snobbish tendency I once had of looking down on ordinary white salt. Salt can be different things. It can be just salt, something you add to the dough or pasta water without giving it much thought. It can also be a taste experience which allows you to find strange creamy tones among the saltiness, or something sharp and powerful, or the taste of sea spray, which is how I find the salt from Ile de Ré and Noirmoutier.

Salt also tells a story about places, a reminder of how important it is to all humankind, and has been for a very long time.

We need salt to survive. Today, the health authorities are concerned that most of us eat too much salt, since it can lead to high blood pressure and therefore increase the risk of heart failure. In the good old days, salt deficiency was just as big a problem. Without salt you can simply die. We still hear stories about what happens when the body's salt level becomes unbalanced, although nowadays it's something that only happens in extreme cases. In the most recent centuries, salt deficiency has only been reported as a major cause of illness during wartime or other catastrophic states of emergency. Salt deficiency saps your energy; you lose your get-up-and-go, quite simply. "A man is no longer capable of tying up a chicken," writes an anonymous seventeenth-century Chinese author, quoted in Robert Multhauf's book *Neptune's Gift*. Multhauf also repeats the hypothesis that salt deficiency was precisely why the southern states lost the American Civil War. According to Multhauf, the hungry, desperate soldiers could mobilize one last effort, but the salt deprivation had left many of them not just unable to tie up chickens, but completely powerless and unable to fight.

Today, clinical salt deficiency particularly affects marathon runners and athletes who drink too much water, or people who have strayed into some diet or other that involves drinking large amounts of water to "cleanse" the body. Consuming too little salt compared to water will eventually make the cells in the body swell up, and lead to dizziness, personality disorders, nausea, and, in the worst cases, death. Following Andy Warhol's death in 1987, his family sued the hospital for poisoning him—with water. They believed he had been given inadequate care, specifically too much water and not enough salt. Skinny Andy, who weighed 128 pounds (58 kg) when he was admitted, had been given so much water he'd swollen up and was 22 pounds (10 kg) heavier when his body was autopsied. He had survived 25 years with an often unhealthy relationship with amphetamines; he'd lived through the AIDS epidemic in New York, and also survived a murder attempt in which a bullet pierced his lung, liver, and stomach. But he died from too much water and too little salt.

BEFORE HUMANS SETTLED in one place, when we still lived as hunters and gatherers, we rarely needed to think about salt. It's unlikely anyone knew what salt was, except that, like us, they had probably noticed that tears are salty, that skin tastes salty when you've sweated, and that salt marks can form where sweat has evaporated. Some people were lucky and lived near a salt source, or—since they lived in different places—had access to one en route.

There was plenty of salt along the coast, and in several places it had accumulated inland, either at salt springs, open fields of rock salt, or in dried-up lakes. But most people got enough salt from their food. There are over 30,000 different edible plants, in addition to all the edible animals, fish, and insects. Common to the early humans was a diet so varied—except during periods of drought, destitution, or other crises—that it provided them with all the nutrients they needed, including salt.

Meat contains more salt than most plants, so in areas with only a few natural salt sources and no access to the sea, humans simply ate more meat. I once visited a family of nomadic reindeer herders in Siberia. It was at the end of March, and they'd eaten nothing but reindeer meat since the first frost of October. Not one vegetable. No salt. But by making use of everything—from the liver and spleen to the eyes, blood, and stomach—they had gotten all the salt they needed. And by eating most of those things raw, they miraculously got the vitamins they needed as well.

In hunter-gatherer societies, the populations adapted to the nutrient intake, which didn't just mean the number of calories available, it also meant salt. In many places, people moved between coastal and inland areas, some of which had very few salt sources and were almost deserted, yet are densely populated today.

When humans settled, our relationship to salt changed—like our relationship to most things, you might say. Instead of wandering over vast areas and eating countless different foods, we stayed in the same place year round, all our lives. We followed a diet consisting of far less meat and only a few basic ingredients. In Europe and the area around the Fertile Crescent (which today includes parts of Iraq, Syria, and Turkey), the staple food was mostly grain. In the other major agricultural area—China—there was millet and rice.

This new diet enabled populations to grow, but it didn't contain enough salt to be enough in itself.

The situation was much the same for animals. When they moved freely and had access to a varied diet, they were able to get what they needed. When European pioneers in North America moved west across the Appalachians, they followed well-established trails, worn into the earth over many years. The explorers were expecting these trails to lead them to large human settlements, perhaps some hidden city, but it turned out they had been created by traveling bison who regularly headed toward the salt licks before returning to graze.

When livestock had been tamed and we had settled down, both humans and animals began eating a more limited diet, and the salt nature offered was no longer sufficient. In this era of agriculture, habitation, and property rights it was no longer possible to move around freely to salt licks now owned by protective neighbors. If you didn't live near the sea, and there were no natural sources of salt where you lived, then it would have to be bought to cover the needs of humans and animals. Agriculture also led to an additional requirement for salt, since it could be used for preserving food. Salt's ability to extract moisture and prevent the growth of bacteria made it possible to keep meat and fish beyond its normal shelf life—which was normally a few days, and perhaps only a few hours during warm periods. In the days before fridges and freezers, before people knew what bacteria were, before hygiene was a natural part of life in the kitchen, salt was the most important preservative.

For these reasons salt became one of the first commodities. Archeologists have found evidence of pearls, precious stones, and tools being traded or exchanged over great distances as far back as a hundred thousand years ago. These were heavily symbolic luxury items; the trade was small in volume and didn't need to be consistent. Salt was the first of life's necessities to become a true commodity; trading it took place on a completely different scale. The demand for salt never ceased; there was a need for a constant and steady supply. Roads were built; camel routes through the desert were established. Those who had salt had something everyone needed. At a time when self-sufficiency was the rule, salt was the exception.

A while back I visited a cathedral of salt in Wieliczka near Krakow, Poland. From the air, Wieliczka looks like a totally normal, moderately—or to be honest slightly less than—charming eastern European town. In the middle of Wieliczka there is an unobtrusive building owned by the salt mine. Once inside, you are led into a spacious hallway, and then through a small side door to a long flight of narrow wooden stairs that wind their way down as far as the eye can see. Hundreds of steps later you end up in a hall, 210 feet (64 m) below ground, where, over the past seven hundred years, a whole subterranean city with more than 180 miles (290 km) of tunnels and over 2,000 rooms and squares have been dug. All due to the excavation of the mine's 13-million-year-old salt deposits. It is a colossal facility, grand and impressive. In the nineteenth and early twentieth centuries the mine even had its own stables down here, deep underground, where the horses lived in darkness without ever breathing fresh air. At its deepest, the mine is more than 1,000 feet (300 m). Its largest room is as tall as a cathedral or the Colosseum, 184 feet (56 m) from floor to ceiling. Another of its grand rooms is a consecrated space, the almost 11,000-square-foot St. Kinga's Chapel, complete with chandeliers and wall reliefs depicting famous biblical scenes. Everything in the chapel is made of salt, from the recreation of the Last Supper, to the relief of Doubting Thomas, and the far newer statue of Pope John Paul II. As you walk through the corridors and look more closely at the floors, walls, and ceilings, you realize that they too are all salt. Quite a few visitors take the liberty of tasting them. The sight of a whole group of Chinese tourists facing the wall with their tongues out is a strange thing to behold. It's like a salty, subterranean, candy castle.

The only reason the walls haven't been excavated too is because they stop the place from collapsing. The mining work ceased in 2007, but several hundred miners still work down here to preserve the intricate structure. When, from time to time, small or large accidents and landslides occur, the entire local community on the surface above will be on the alert. A mine collapse wouldn't only be a disaster for those working down there and the many people dependent on the tourism the ancient mine attracts—very many of Wieliczka's 20,000 inhabitants live right on top of it. The city's revenue has, for centuries, depended on removing the very foundations it stands on.

Wieliczka is a triumph of human creativity and engineering, like an eighth wonder hidden underground. But despite Wieliczka's seven-hundred-year history—and although Copernicus was the mine's first salt tourist over five hundred years ago, curious about the monumental excavation project—it wasn't until the late 1800s and early 1900s that mining technology had advanced enough for it to really take off. During most of world history, salt has been a valuable resource to which we have had limited access.

But the need for salt has always been there. Long before the mine was excavated, the people in the area used its salt. There is evidence that 6,000 years ago, the inhabitants of what is today Wieliczka produced salt by boiling the water that ran from the springs above the mines. It was a technique used in many places, a reliable although incredibly laborious way of making salt, since it required large quantities of fuel. One of the salts in my collection, a smoked French salt called Sel d'Egersund, is named after the town of Egersund in southwest Norway; and I have another, from the same manufacturer, with the slightly more commercial name Sel Viking—viking salt. As far as I can tell, there is nothing Norwegian about them. It's possible that salt was boiled along the Norwegian coast, and it may have had a rather smoky taste, but it was a production defect people just lived with, until someone realized it perhaps gave an added quality.

Mined salt is called rock salt. What we call sea salt is extracted using various methods from seawater. The salt my son found on the rocks at Paternoster on the west coast of South Africa occurred naturally. Salt like this does exist, but it's relatively scarce. There are plenty of boulders and an equally wild Atlantic Ocean at the southern tip of Norway, where my family has a small farm, but it's extremely rare for us to find salt. The climate isn't conducive for sustained evaporation. It rains too much, and during the summer, when you can sometimes be lucky enough to get several days or even weeks of sun, the waves are seldom rough enough to splash large amounts of seawater onto the rocks.

On another family trip to Paternoster, we came across some salt flats just north of the town. Not rocks this time but a marshy landscape separated from the beach by tall sand dunes. At certain times of the year, when the weather is at its worst, or if the sand dunes move, gaps can form in between, which allow the seawater to flood through. The water then gets trapped and slowly evaporates. Around the edges of these sand dunes, the salt was beginning to dry, forming a crust in some places, big lumps in others. Out in the middle of the shallow salt flats, two flamingos walked where salt had been harvested throughout the ages, first by animals, later by humans.

There was once a salt source like this close to Rome. The area at the mouth of the river Tiber, roughly where Fiumicino Airport is today, was originally salt flats, and when Rome was founded it must have looked similar to the marshy landscape at Paternoster. A northerly current in the Tyrrhenian Sea sweeps along the coast of Ostia, and the Tiber has been leaving sediment there since time immemorial, creating a delta-like lowland area. The high tides, storms, and constant pressure from the Tyrrhenian left trapped seawater, which in turn evaporated to leave salt. This salt could then be harvested throughout the late summer and the autumn.

"Nothing is more useful than salt and sunshine," wrote Pliny the Elder in his *Natural History* in the first century AD. Before mining made it possible to extract huge quantities of salt, these natural salt flats were the source of most of the salt available to humans. As the demand for salt only grew, techniques were developed to increase production at the salt flats. Ostia's salt flats were gradually developed to incorporate locks, canals, and salt collection pools. Below Erice, Sicily, where our enlightening—although for food snobs and salt-collectors rather depressing—salt-tasting workshop was held, lie the famous Trapani salt flats. It is a place where, with a little imagination, you can picture how Rome's salt flats looked when they came under human control, and were not only harvested but actively run as a garden.

The Trapani salt flats are now a UNESCO World Heritage Site, covering almost 2,500 acres and divided into hundreds of pools. At high tide, seawater is let in at regular intervals and channeled into the pools. The water supply is then shut off to achieve the same result as the storms and unforeseen flooding had done previously, just in an easy and more predictable way. In the months prior to the autumn rains, small, white salt mountains stand on the flat, barren marshland. To a visitor from the north, they look like snowdrifts defying the arid surroundings.

Its proximity to the salt flats at the mouth of the Tiber was one reason why Rome, although secluded, held a degree of strategic importance from the very start. The first road to and from Rome went from the coast through the city and beyond to the inland areas, before ending at Ascoli and Ancona on the east side of the Italian peninsula. The road was called Via Salaria—the salt road—and was, as its name indicates, used to transport salt to the country's interior.

Rome wasn't built in a day. It didn't grow primarily because of kings, generals, or emperors, but through a combination of human and natural conditions. One of these was its access to salt—the world's first regular commodity, and for much of human history the most important one as well.

Because everyone needs salt, it has always been important to the authorities. As early as 508 BC, Rome chose to take control of salt formally by establishing a state salt monopoly, just as they would start controlling other parts of the trade and distribution of food later on. It wasn't enough that salt was traded via Rome, and that its merchants, and therefore the rest of society, profited from the business. In order to avoid the state's authority being undermined by rising prices, untrustworthy traders, or the people owning the salt flats, the control of salt needed to be absolute.

While conquerors could get an income by exploiting the local people—from looting and robbing, basically—a lasting way of founding a state relied on getting an income from its own citizens through various forms of tax. In some cases it was for the common good, as we know it today, with government-funded infrastructure and services, but originally it was just as likely to have been what we now call exploitation, extracting as much as possible from the populace to fund the whims and follies of those in power: palaces, parties, and wars. The problem, from the rulers' point of view, was finding a tax that could be collected from a population that had no income-generating work, where most people didn't own the land they worked or the house they lived in, and lived in a form of natural economy. The solution was taxing salt, and by controlling its trade, the state could also control the price and take a sky-high profit. Salt tax is probably the oldest tax there is, and historically the most unpopular.

During the French Revolution in 1789, one cause was the revolt against France's salt tax, *la gabelle du sel*, which had been introduced in the thirteenth century. At its most oppressive, the French salt tax had been more than a government scheme to control trade that led to sky-high prices. It was the most unfair tax of all, a kind of poll tax, equally high for all regardless of their financial means. Periodically it required all citizens to buy a certain amount of salt from the authorities at a price the authorities had set. There were even separate rules for what you could use the salt for. If you were going to use it to cure meat, you might have to pay extra tax. If you were accused of salt fraud, *faux saunage*, you could be prosecuted and sent to prison or—in serious cases—sentenced to death. Different rules and taxes in different parts of the country meant that the price varied enormously. While one sou could buy you 3⅓ lb (1.5 kg) of salt in Brittany—which had negotiated an exemption from the salt tax when it was united with the rest of France —it would only buy you just under 3 ounces (75 g) in Poitou a little further south. For many of the revolutionaries climbing the barricades their main interests were not primarily the philosophical ideas of enlightenment or the lofty principles of liberty, equality, and fraternity. The riots were equally motivated by their outrage at the high price of bread, and the desire to have salt in their food.

The Romans and the French were not alone in using this form of taxation. On the other side of the world, in China, salt tax and strict governmental control of salt were introduced as early as the Han dynasty in the 100s BC. For periods, salt tax accounted for more than half of China's state revenue, and it is said to have provided most of the funds used for building its Great Wall. In India, the British introduced a brutal salt tax and state-controlled monopoly in the nineteenth century as a way to finance the running of the empire. It was seen as very unfair, to put it mildly. The British took over the saltworks, shut them down, and posted soldiers to guard them from people who might help themselves to the salt. They had moved on from the idea of simply taxing and controlling salt production where it was. In practice, they banned Indian salt production altogether, which meant that Indians could only eat salt imported from England, and had to pay far more for it than it would cost to produce it themselves, even significantly more than it cost in England. It was a way of achieving a trade balance, a form of compensation for England's imports of fabric and tea.

And what could the Indians do? They were bound by British supremacy. This has—almost since the dawn of time—been the problem for people subjected to a state power that has exploited them or ruled without their consent. At the start of the twentieth century, Indian citizens began protesting against British rule. They did not want to be a jewel in a crown; what they wanted was to rule themselves. A group of well-educated intellectuals who saw themselves as the country's future leaders formed the Congress Party.

They made pamphlets about reforming the state administration and promoted their desire for legislative change, referencing political philosophers such as John Locke and John Stuart Mill.

One of them, Mohandas Gandhi—later referred to by the honorary title Mahatma, meaning "great soul"—decided to approach the struggle for independence from a different angle. He focused on everyday issues, things that mattered to those who didn't read pamphlets or philosophical theories. On March 12, 1930, he embarked on a 24-day-long peaceful protest march. The act of rebellion at the center of the whole march was the boiling of seawater and collecting of salt lumps from the shore. This was something people had done throughout the ages, but it had become a punishable offense under colonial law. The salt protests spread throughout the country, leading to the arrest of more than 60,000 people, including Gandhi. Today, the event is considered the beginning of the end for the British Empire.

The control of salt is an example of early government control that we might smile wryly at today. Imagine a world where salt is taxed and controlled using the full force of the law! It seems so weird. Salt tax and salt monopolies belong to societies far from ours both historically and geographically. Now, we grumble instead about the tax on gas, tobacco, and alcohol. On the one hand, we don't like having to pay at all; on the other, we have a vague understanding that it's in both our own and the community's best interests. But taxing salt? It seems absurd.

So I was surprised to hear that the Italian salt monopoly wasn't completely abolished until 1975. An article from the start of the century in the British magazine *The Spectator* describes the monopoly in all its officious absurdity:

The whole lengthy coast-line of Italy is most rigidly guarded by tens of thousands of coastguards and police to prevent any person whatsoever taking a cupful of water out of the sea out of fear of the salt monopoly being injured. And so well is the sea guarded, and so heavy are the penalties for infringing the law, that no saltwater is ever used by peasants who may live on the seashore . . . On account of this Salt-tax, Italy cannot fairly make use of her fisheries, and the importation of salt fish is enormous. On the other hand, thousands of men receive small salaries and a uniform and sword to walk about the coast and enforce the law—a most healthy, if rather idle, career.

China's salt monopoly was only partially abolished in 2017, by which point it had been in place for more than 2,100 years. Salt tax accounted for more than 5 percent of China's state revenue until as recent as 1950.

When we look at why certain foods have become so important to the history of mankind, it's normal to search for rational-sounding explanations. The result of this is that food is often seen as just calories and nutrients. And that's often sensible. We began using salt because we have a physiological need for it, then became even more dependent on salt when we began keeping livestock, since they have the same, or even greater, need for it; and salt's ability to preserve food made it indispensable. Today, most of the salt extracted is used for industrial purposes. All these reasons are correct and important. But aren't we forgetting something essential here?

There's another reason, which is so obvious that we take it for granted. We see it without noticing it, like the salt shaker on the table in front of me. On man's journey—from hunter-gatherer in the wild, to today's enlightened tourist at a restaurant table in a city so ancient you could be convinced that it is eternal—so many changes have occurred that we can't quite relate to the people of the past as though they were like us. We risk thinking that the wants, needs, and preferences of latter-day people were different to those we feel ourselves, those that govern us now.

So let me share an account that may shed some light on man's dependence on salt, a detour to something quite central. In the seventeenth century, the Russian Orthodox Church carried out a number of reforms, including a decision that members of this more modern church should start crossing themselves with three fingers, not two, as they had done before. The spelling of "hallelujah" and "Jesus" was also changed to bring it more in line with the original Greek text in the Bible. Moreover, religious processions were reformed, requiring you to move counterclockwise, not clockwise as before. All dramatic changes—for those interested in such things.

A group of conservative congregations, people we would now call fundamentalists, opposed the reforms so vehemently that they broke with the Church. They called themselves Old Believers, and for centuries to come insisted on maintaining the archaic rituals and old-fashioned practices, walking clockwise in defiance of modernity. The early Old Believers were persecuted and harassed, and sometimes had to pay double tax. The men were charged an extra fee because they had such long beards. Nevertheless, the group remained a not insignificant minority well into the twentieth century. It's quite possible that there were hundreds of thousands of Old Believers living in remote farming communities in Russia, Ukraine, and the Baltics.

In 1936, the Soviet Communist regime launched another brutal wave of persecution of Old Believers. After seeing his brother killed, Karp Lykov, an Old Believer and family father, decided to escape with his wife and children from the village of Perm on the European side of the Ural mountains. Where could they find safety? For several years, the Lykov family moved further and further into the taiga until they finally ended up in a clearing not far from the Mongolian border. There, in one of the most isolated parts of the world, they survived by hunting and growing the few seeds they had brought with them.

When their pots rusted and eventually fell apart, they had to make cooking pans out of bark. They insulated the house they had built with bark, they clothed themselves with bark, and their diet included large amounts of bark. Overall there was an abundance of bark, but very little else. Instead of expanding, their garden shrank. One summer all the carrots they had grown were eaten by wild animals; another year snow fell in June and destroyed the entire harvest. The following year, however, they found one surviving rye grain, and from this one grain they grew one ear of rye, which had eighteen new grains, which they used to slowly rebuild their grain store. After that, things worsened. The 1950s were lean years. They ate what they could, including rowanberry leaves and bark. One particularly harsh winter, the mother chose to abstain from food to ensure that the children had enough to survive on; she died.

In just a few decades the family regressed thousands of years to something approaching a kind of natural state. Their old-fashioned variant of Christianity had also become increasingly eclectic. They lived in nature, and off nature. Karp's son Dimitri hunted barefoot, even in the middle of winter. They lacked proper weapons and were reliant on finding ways to scare animals into pitfalls. It was, one can assume with a high degree of certainty, a hard life.

It went on like this for 46 years, until 1981, when they were discovered almost by chance by a group of geologists flying over the area in a helicopter.

It was a dramatic encounter with the outside world. Two of the children, born after the family's escape from Perm, had never seen other people before. The family had taken just one book with them, the Bible, which they had read more and more selectively, and with increasing difficulty. But despite the lack of most things, they seemed content and in relatively good health. At first, they weren't interested in help. They refused to accept anything from the outside world, be it food or equipment, and carried on living more or less as they had done. The only thing Karp, the head of the family, wanted on everyone's behalf was salt. Living without salt, he said, had been the worst thing about life in the wilderness. "True torture," he called it.

This yearning for salt had not been about necessity or anything physiological. Having returned to a kind of hunter-gatherer exist-ence, they had never suffered from clinical salt deficiency; their varied diet had most likely ensured that they got what little salt the body needs to prevent illness. But for Karp, who had grown up with salt, every meal out in the wilderness had been a reminder of what the food could have tasted like. For him, salt had become one of life's essentials, for the same reason that there's a salt shaker in front of me on the restaurant table: we have become addicted to the taste. What's worth its salt, is salt.

PASTA

What would Italian food be without pasta? It is almost unimaginable. The regular pasta dish—nothing showy or grand—is what most Italians eat every day. Often twice a day. A mountain of pasta for lunch, and pasta as *primi* for dinner. It is confirmation that everything is as it should be, and that they are Italians.

La Carbonara is an institution as well as a restaurant, with a large capacity and—as is often the case with such big restaurants—an enormous menu. It has page after page of dishes with a clear emphasis on *primi*, the starchy first course, where you'll find *bucatini all'amatriciana*—long, hollow pasta tubes with tomato, guanciale, and pecorino—cured pork jowls and hard sheep's milk cheese. Like so many recipes this too has its origins in the countryside, in this case Amatrice, a mountain village in the province of Lazio, 100 miles (160 km) northeast of Rome. You will also find the minimalistic *pasta alla checca*, which comes with tomato and not much else; and *spaghetti aglio, olio e peperoncini*, an even simpler variant consisting of spaghetti, garlic, oil, and chili. There is linguine with anchovies and tomatoes, the classic carbonara, and *rigatoni alla gricia*, which is almost like carbonara, but without eggs. In addition, the menu offers dishes that shouldn't really be served here, such as northern Italian specialties like *spaghetti alle vongole*, a Venetian dish with carpet shells that was once considered unthinkable to serve inland out of sight of the Adriatic, or even the Venetian Lagoon.

Also among the *primis* you'll find one lonely risotto dish and one gnocchi dish. It is pasta that dominates in Rome.

Since I'm actually at La Carbonara, it has to *be* pasta carbonara, or *mezzi rigatoni alla carbonara*, as it's called in the menu. It's what I almost always end up with, after pretending to be carefully considering all the other options my carbonara addiction invariably wins. Angelo puts a plate of steaming pasta on the table, as he's done thousands of times before, and, with a solemn, deliberate flicker of the hand, rotates the dish so that the tiny restaurant logo is directly facing me, at twelve o'clock on the lip of the plate. To me, this is the very taste of Rome: golden pasta with the aroma of fried pork fat, melted pecorino, and a little sting of black pepper. I simply cannot visit the city without eating carbonara, usually several times.

In the film *Un americano a Roma* (An American in Rome) from 1954, we meet Nando Moriconi, a young man dazzled by the idea of America. He knows nothing about the country far away across the Atlantic, other than what he's seen in the movies, and he dreams about the Wild West, fast cars, sheriffs, and skyscrapers. Nor can he speak any English, so he just mimics the sounds in a ridiculous quasi-English way. In the film's most famous scene, he comes home late from the cinema after playing cops and robbers in the streets. His parents have already gone to bed, but his mother has left him a large bowl of spaghetti—*maccharoni*, which at the time was the collective term for pasta—and there's a bottle of red wine, a traditional straw-covered fiasco, on the table. Nando sneers at the food and pushes it aside. "Macaroni, this stuff is for cart drivers! I'm not eating macaroni, I'm American!" Instead, he makes what he imagines is a real American sandwich: a mixture of white bread, yogurt, marmalade, jam, and mustard, which he pours milk over. "That's how the Americans beat the Apaches," he righteously declares before taking the first bite of the sandwich—which he promptly spits out.

The scene ends, as expected, with him throwing himself upon his mother's pasta and eating ravenously. The film is charming, outdated, and overacted. But it lives on nevertheless. The picture of Nando with his mouth full of pasta hangs on the walls in the homes of thousands of ordinary Italians and in countless restaurants. No matter how much he pretends to be something else, he is first and foremost Italian. And Italians, both cart drivers and others alike, eat pasta.

This sense of bloated self-satisfaction at the heart of Italian culture was what led Filippo Tommaso Marinetti, the leader of the Futurist movement, to launch a full-frontal assault on Italian gastronomy in the 1930s. Of all Marinetti's eccentric schemes, he is probably still best remembered for his proposal to ban pasta. It sounds like a joke, a bizarre provocation. And while it was undoubtedly the latter, it was certainly not the former.

F. T. Marinetti, as he called himself, was born in Alexandria, Egypt, in 1876. After giving up his plans to become a lawyer in favor of art, he settled in Paris, where he wrote experimental poems and hung around with the artists and writers, among them the famous sculptor Constantin Brâncuși. He was a carefree playboy and lived on family money, of which there was plenty. The turning point came—according to the myths he so readily constructed around himself—on October 15, 1908, when he was involved in a car accident driving his new four-cylinder Fiat sports car. Marinetti escaped relatively unharmed from the incident and wasn't particularly shaken by it. On the contrary, this artistic rich man's son was in love and fascinated with what he had experienced, entirely convinced that the accident had given him an insight into the future and what it could be: a place of tempo, power, and exhaust fumes, of metal and brutal contrasts—everything Marinetti wanted from a modern world.

In February the following year, Marinetti launched "The Manifesto of Futurism" in the newspaper *Gazzetta dell'Emilia* in Bologna and the French newspaper *Le Figaro*. In the manifesto's introduction, he describes his car accident: after a long night of conversation beneath "lamps whose brass cupolas are bright as our souls, because like them they were illuminated by the internal glow of electric hearts," he and his friends had driven off on the country road where he encountered

two cyclists disapproving of me and tottering in front of me like two persuasive but contradictory reasons. Their stupid swaying got in my way. What a bore! Pouah! I stopped short, and in disgust hurled myself — vlan! — head over heels in a ditch. Oh, maternal ditch, half full of muddy water! A factory gutter! I savored a mouthful of strengthening muck which recalled the black teat of my Sudanese nurse!

You don't need to have attended metaphor school to understand that Marinetti saw Futurism as a renaissance, a rebirth. A new world born of oil and sludge. The cyclists were old-fashioned Italians, slow-moving and forever bickering, blocking the road, and the time had come for them to make way for the sports car of progress.

After this, Marinetti embarked on a grand and absurd nation-wrecking-and-rebuilding project. In another manifesto he launched a scathing attack on Venice, proposing to have the entire city paved and fill "the small, stinking canals with the rubble from the old, collapsing and leprous palaces." He hated Rome at least as much. According to Marinetti, the two cities were prostitutes, and their inhabitants "pimps of the past."

Most of what Marinetti said and wrote was of little interest to anyone beyond a fringe group of manifesto-reading intellectuals. He was often looked upon as a curiosity, much to his own frustration. Despite many spectacularly fanciful attempts, he failed to engage the masses until 1930, when he launched the *Manifesto della cucina futurista* (Manifesto of Futurist Cooking), where, with typical braggadocio, he ridiculed the Italians for their dependence on tradition on a subject they were extremely passionate about. His manifesto presented the plans for a brand-new cuisine based not on ancient recipes and local ingredients but on speed and power. No knives or forks, just technical equipment that would crush the food and create new textures. It was crazy and visionary, a precursor to the molecular gastronomy that ravaged the early 2000s. However, the idea of a Futurist kitchen turned heads primarily because of a proposal to ban pasta. Marinetti saw the Italians' unquestioning love of pasta as an "absurd Italian religion." To him, pasta symbolized everything that was wrong: it made Italians lazy, unimaginative, fat—and, perhaps worst of all for the cantankerous protofascist, peaceful.

The food stunt gained a huge amount of attention, and was covered by newspapers all over the country. Even foreign newspapers wrote about the conflict in the home of pasta, one writing that it all "sounds about as rational as starting a liberation front in Leeds to abolish Yorkshire pudding." Marinetti appreciated the attention, but was especially happy about the social engagement that followed. With every angry letter to the editor, every petition, and every public threat, his fame increased. A group of housewives in L'Aquila collected signatures and wrote protest letters in support of pasta. The mayor of Naples attacked Marinetti, claiming it was an "undisputed truth" that the angels in paradise ate nothing but pasta and tomato sauce, to which Marinetti replied that this confirmed his assumption that the afterlife was intolerably boring. He was a man who loved taunting people, the kind of guy who saw defeat as victory and defamation as vindication. After being challenged to a duel and seriously injured, he wore his scar with pride, as proof that his words had power.

But he never got rid of pasta. It is the heart of Italian culture. Today's Italians can laugh condescendingly at Nando in *An American in Rome* and sigh wearily at how caricatured and stupid he is, yet they recognize themselves in the pasta scene. I've met Italians traveling abroad who go dewy-eyed when they find a pack of Barilla Spaghetti n.5 in a grocery store.

It's almost impossible to imagine two parties more at odds than Marinetti and the Accademia Italiana della Cucina, the Italian organization that protects the civilization of the table; it is a kind of gastronomic version of the World Wildlife Fund. While the WWF works for species diversity and the protection of endangered animals, the academy fights the abuse of culinary shrines and to protect endangered traditional dishes. When there are rumors about someone using cream in the *lasagna alla bolognese*, or Chinese rice in the risotto, or foreign cheese on pizza, the academy springs into action with cries of protest.

Caring for such things isn't about being hung up on details, they claim; it's about the essence of food itself. And more than that: food is the essence of life, they say. "Cooking is in fact one of the most profound forms of expression of a nation's culture," reads the academy's manifesto. "It is the fruit of the history and life of its inhabitants." The academy sees it as their duty to safeguard taste, and therefore "the very identity of a people." They are fighting against simplification, decline, and reinvention.

Surprisingly, Marinetti and the Accademia Italiana della Cucina agree on one major point: they both believe that civilization of the table is the key to understanding Italy. And, to Marinetti's consternation: in the middle of this Italian table is a bowl of steaming pasta.

There are many stories about how pasta came to Italy. The most popular, which most people have heard, is that Marco Polo brought it back from China. The story goes like this: Polo and his fellow travelers, including a Venetian by the name of Spaghetti, made landfall on the Chinese coast. And in a small village, Spaghetti learned the art of mixing flour and water and rolling it into long sticks, which had a long shelf life and tasted delicious when cooked in salted water. He took the innovation home to Italy, "and before long a similar dish, made from home-grown wheat, could be found on everyone's tables." It's a fantastic tale that unfortunately has no roots in reality whatsoever. Marco Polo was widely known for his self-promoting yarns, and it is said that children ran after him in the streets and shouted: "Mr. Polo, tell us a new lie," partly mocking, partly hoping for a new, unbelievable story. But although he rarely shied from telling fanciful tales that would make his adventures look more significant, he never claimed to have discovered pasta in any of them. He only refers to pasta when recounting how he saw a tree that was used to make something resembling pasta—sago palm perhaps, from which the Chinese would extract a starchy flour to make noodles. From what I've found, the imaginative story of pasta's journey from China to Italy probably originated in a 1929 issue of the *Macaroni Journal*, the trade magazine for American pasta makers. The story was part of the advertising campaign of the Keystone Macaroni Company in Pennsylvania, a story not more truthful than that of the Green Giant used to promote canned corn, and it was never meant to be taken literally. But it quickly spread, as good stories often do, and after being retold often enough, it came to be seen as true.

Had it been the case that Marco Polo and his imaginary fellow traveler Spaghetti had brought pasta home from China, it would have been of scant significance, for it would by no means have been the first pasta in Europe. The Romans and Greeks ate an early variant of lasagne as early as 2,000 years ago: flat plates of dough that were baked in the oven and were called *laganum* or *tractum*. In their book *Pasta: The Story of a Universal Food*, Serventi and Sabban write about *itrium*, another type of flour-and-water dough which was fried or boiled in pots and eaten in Palestine during the fourth century. At the same time, or perhaps a little later, the Arabs developed another type of pasta, *itriyya*, which was shaped into long threads, and is therefore considered spaghetti's most direct predecessor. The Arabs brought the technique to Sicily sometime in the tenth century—and as early as the twelfth century, long before Marco Polo's time, this specialty was being made and exported in large volumes to mainland Italy and several other Christian countries. In northern Italy, the first documented source of pasta comes from Genoa, "a barrel of *macaroni*," listed among the property of the deceased soldier Ponzio Bastone in 1279, almost twenty years before Marco Polo returned from his travels.

Seen from one angle, pasta is a fairly universal concept. Making pasta was a way of storing the flour that was otherwise in danger of going moldy or being eaten by flour beetles. In that sense, there's a close relationship between pasta and several other flour-and-water mixtures. Poor countries like Norway made flatbread out of whole wheat or simpler grains like barley, but this was probably used quite similarly to pasta. Soup or broth was served with pasta, or with flatbread that had been softened. It's hard to say when the tradition of cooking pasta until it is *al dente* came about, but it was more recently. Very old cookbooks often state the cooking time to be thirty minutes, sometimes considerably longer. These recipes should carry a warning—"do not try this at home"—because you'll end up with something halfway between pasta and porridge.

It's also possible to claim that pasta as we know it didn't exist before Italy existed, in other words, not until well into the 1800s. I would argue that what's special about pasta isn't that it's a mixture of flour and water. You can eat couscous in North Africa, weird and wonderful noodle desserts in the Middle East, wheat noodles in northern China, and surprising Japanese varieties. Germany and several other nearby countries also traditionally serve cooked dough—either dried or fresh—in various forms. But today no one feels like they have eaten a pasta dish after eating pork knuckle with spätzle in Munich, a bowl of ramen in Tokyo, meat broth with flatbread in Norway, or noodle soup in Thailand. Pasta is, as the academy and Marinetti—and, may I add, all reasonable people— agree, Italian pasta.

It's even possible to claim that Italy didn't exist before pasta. When Giuseppe Garibaldi united Italy in the 1850s and '60s, it was not a divided nation longing to be whole. The boot-shaped peninsula and Sicilian football consisted of several different king- doms and provinces, many of which hadn't been under the same administration since they were all part of the Roman Empire. Some neighbors felt a degree of kinship, but not everyone felt alike. They spoke different languages, had different customs, and looked differ- ent. The northern Italians saw the southern Italians as "Africans," not compatriots.

One of the things that made most Italians finally accept that they were unified, and gradually made them feel as if they belonged to the same people, was that they began eating the same thing. It was a process in which pasta—and to some extent pizza—played a central role. In the mid-1800s, pasta and pizza were mostly regional specialties, poor man's food from Naples and the surrounding areas. After Italy's unification, immigrants from the country's poor south flocked to cities in the north searching for work. They took their favorite food with them—and poor man's food soon became everyone's favorite. As John Dickie writes in his book *Delizia*, one of the most remarkable traits of the Italians' love of food today is how democratic it is. In the past, the rich and the poor, the people living in the cities and the countryside, lived on completely different diets; today it's likely that their children and grandchildren share the same knowledge and appreciation of tasty cooking. Everyone dreams about the same bowl of pasta, although the sauce varies slightly from region to region.

When the Accademia Italiana della Cucina talks about "the civilization of the table," it is a sincerely meant provocation. To put the table and the meal at the center of Italian culture breaks from the dominant view that constructs a pyramid of civilization with art, religion, and written language on top—and food at the bottom, as a necessity. Food is the body's fuel, while art is associated with the spirit, intellect, and culture. The academy's overriding argument seems to be that food is also culture, and that it has an equal—if not greater—potential to bind people together and be an expression of mankind's need to create. Not everyone goes to the theater, museum, or opera, but we all have to eat, and having shared food culture helps define who we are. Italians are defined more by pasta than by Puccini and Michelangelo.

Fellini believed that life is a combination of magic and pasta, both of which are found in a bowl of carbonara. I have a minor masterpiece before me, a dish that almost defies nature. On the one hand, it's so rich, so full of sauce—or whatever you want to call it—yet there's almost no sauce when you've eaten all the pasta. La Carbonara serves the dish with small rigatoni, ridged pasta tubes, to which the sauce clings as if they were magnetic. Golden carbonara is a great comfort food when you're down, it serves as an energy pack when you're hungry, it's food you can eat with the kids or on a date— both informal and sophisticated at once. The recipe is simple, but it's difficult to perfect. When you make it yourself, it tends to become too viscous, which can make it sickly and nauseating. Otherwise it can easily get so hot that the egg coagulates and becomes grainy. The sauce can be too overwhelming, or there can be too little of it. And it's never, ever as good as the one they serve at La Carbonara.

The restaurant's history dates back more than a hundred years. Federico Salomone was a coal merchant in Rione Ponte, the area near Ponte Sant'Angelo south of the Tiber. And while he sold coal to the neighbors, his wife Domenica cooked food, which she served to the local workers. Over time, Domenica's eatery became a local institution. It was the end of the 1800s and Rome had just become the capital of a newly unified Italy. The city was growing after 1,500 years of more or less continual decline and decay. Noble families from around the country were moving in, many of them building their new homes in and around Rione Ponte. There was more of everybody: more workers, officials, soldiers, and businessmen. In 1861, the population of Rome was less than 200,000. A hundred years later, it had risen to over 2 million.

Eventually, the food became more important than the coal, and when Federico died Domenica began running a restaurant full time. She expanded and professionalized, but to honor her late husband, she kept the name which had always hung outside, "Il Carbonaro"—the coal merchant. Several decades later, her daughter Andreina took over the business. The place was by then a proper restaurant with a full menu with several options—it was respectability bordering on the fashionable. The establishment even had their own cutlery, so the guests no longer needed to bring their own, as was customary in the old days. The restaurant did well, and in the wake of Italy's capitulation after the Second World War, Andreina moved it to its current location on the north side of Piazza Campo de' Fiori. To honor her father—and probably to continue using an established brand—she too kept the name, but with one minor change: it was adjusted from Il Carbonaro to La Carbonara. The restaurant—now run by Dominica's granddaughter Maria, her husband Dario, and their children—is known for being a custodian of the original and much-debated recipe for pasta carbonara. It is simple in its genius, although it's hard to agree on what the recipe really is, as is often the case with Italian food. The key to success with Italian cooking doesn't lie with the best chef—as it does with French cooking—but with whoever can prove that theirs is the original.

One of the most seductive and occasionally frustrating things about Italy and Italians is their obsession with food, and how rarely they agree. If you talk to an Italian foodie about an Italian dish, she will most certainly have a very fixed opinion about how it should be made and where it comes from. If you're talking with two people, they will normally disagree completely—and I have often wondered why. One explanation could be that Italians, despite their definitive Italianness, do not yet have a common narrative, one unifying story, about their country. Instead they have a range of locally patriotic mini-narratives—the sauce on the pasta, if you will. They hold their traditions sacred, even when they are quite new; yes, even when they seem inferior to their neighbor's traditions, just because that is "how things have always been."

The first time I was working in Italy, during the 1990s, restaurant kitchens all over Europe had been recently invaded by pesto. It was like an epidemic—barely a dish was served without this green herbal purée. And it wasn't restricted to Italian food. Pesto was used *on* everything and *for* everything. It was used as a marinade for monkfish and for lamb. Tiny green drops of pesto were used on salads and fried fish, and as a semi-artistic flourish on the side of the plate. Pesto made its way into sandwiches and pizza toppings. It was there at lavish parties and simple weekday meals. It had become, for the urban middle class, what ketchup was to the world of fast food.

I WAS THEREFORE thoroughly pesto-marinated myself when I arrived in the homeland of the green mixture, where they were quite oblivious to how important it had become abroad. The first place I ate after crossing the border into Italy was in a small village not far from Genoa, where I was served the best pesto ever. "This is how it should taste! This is what it's like in Italy!" And in the following days, when I was in doubt about what to eat for lunch or dinner, I ordered the same thing, pasta with pesto. The safe choice when the house specialties threatened strange and bitter vegetables, anchovies, or offal, stuff I wasn't yet comfortable with. But at my next stop, a couple of hundred miles away, the pesto was already different; no longer rich and full-bodied or abundant with parmesan and pine nuts. It must have been a mistake, I thought, or bad luck with my choice of restaurant; but at the next place it was different again, miserly and thin, and with yet another twist: it contained a combination of what might have been a particularly astringent basil heavily supplemented with oregano and parsley. A local variation, perhaps? Hardly an improvement. And so it continued until, somewhere outside Rome, I was served boiled pasta that had acquired green freckles from a sprinkling of dried basil, and it had also been drowned in olive oil. The parmesan was served on the side, but it was sharp and salty, not at all like other parmesans. It was terrible. Had I been in a restaurant anywhere but Italy I would have sent it back. Here I just remained quiet, disappointed, and appalled. "It's because the pesto you're used to is *pesto alla genovese*—the pesto from Genoa," I was later told. "That's the best one. You have to understand that other regions have different pestos!" No, that is not understandable! Why in the world can't you just use the same recipe? Why doesn't everyone just want to make the good version, the one with basil, pine nuts, garlic, parmesan, and oil?

It's the same with carbonara. Even in Italy it can come in all sorts of weird varieties. Often it will be nothing but pasta swimming in a creamy sauce. Other times it will be dry, almost crumbly, as though someone has made it out of spite, to prove what a bad idea it was. If carbonara falls victim to a chef trying to make "the best carbonara in town" who goes heavy with the guanciale, and adds plenty of egg yolk or an extra-mature pecorino, things can really go wrong. It will be good, sure, but in a Pepsi challenge too-much-of-a-good-thing-way: a chef's generosity can easily make it a little nauseating as a result. Here at La Carbonara, they do it right, with a mix of moderation and authenticity. They serve hundreds, perhaps thousands of portions every week, and it's such second nature that the result is silky-soft and smooth.

Pasta alla carbonara is a pillar of Italy's most respected non-physical structure: *la cucina autentica*—the sum of the various national and regional specialties that make up Italian cuisine. *Pasta alla carbonara* is from Rome, and should contain guanciale, eggs, pepper, pasta, and pecorino. If you're lacking any of this is, it is not *pasta alla carbonara*. If you've added something, it is not *pasta alla carbonara* either. End of discussion!

When making carbonara, you are making Rome's most important dish, so it would be wrong to use parmesan—*parmeggiano reggiano*—which comes from the Emilia-Romagna region around Parma. In Rome they use pecorino, a cheese made from ewe's milk. This cheese, which gave the pesto I ate just outside Rome its questionably sharp taste, is what gives carbonara an extra dimension. I take a bite of the pasta to see if I can taste it. Sometimes, when Romans make really hardcore versions of the dish *cacio pepe*—pasta with cheese and pepper—you'll get a slight whiff of sheep and barns when the plate comes to the table. You don't get that with my carbonara, although the taste does have an extra depth to it, something funky among the mild flavors and grease. Using pancetta or—God forbid—bacon is also a sin. It *must* be guanciale—pork jowl—which gives you the sweetest and crispiest fat. When I stand on the terrace of my apartment around four or five o'clock, I can smell the guanciale being fried by the chefs at La Carbonara. For several hours, the smell of pork fat drifts gently over the rooftops. You won't get that taste from cheating and cooking the cured meat on a baking tray in the oven, like sloppy chefs do.

One of the many stories about the origin of carbonara is actually about La Carbonara, from the time when Federico and Domenica ran their dual purpose coal-sales-and-restaurant business. The story goes that carbonara is a dish typically served in the families of coal sellers because this power diet was especially suited for the hard-working coal workers; and their food would regularly get speckled with coal dust while they ate, so the pepper is there as an homage to the dish's humble origins.

To claim that pasta carbonara is one of the world's most famous and popular dishes is no exaggeration. But the various "carbonara" of the world are rarely like the strictly composed Roman version. The Accademia Italiana della Cucina has published a list of what it believes are the "most commonly falsified" Italian recipes, and the supreme champion is pasta carbonara. "If your boyfriend makes carbonara with pancetta or bacon instead of guanciale, break up," is a piece of playful Italian relationship advice. From this, in an Italian context, fairly uncontroversial starting point, it continues: "If your boyfriend makes carbonara with garlic, break up. If your boyfriend makes carbonara with parsley, break up. If your boyfriend makes carbonara with onions, break up. If your boyfriend makes carbonara from a box or packet, get a restraining order."

Pasta carbonara spread to the rest of Europe via England. The River Café in London—the restaurant where Jamie Oliver trained and was discovered—was one of the first restaurants to present Italian cuisine as more than just spaghetti with tomato sauce in a restaurant with red-checked tablecloths and candles sticking out of fiasco bottles. On the banks of the Thames, they introduced an idealized Italy where the food was cooked in a wood-fired oven and the olive oil was always virginal. They served hundred-pound-a-bottle wines with simple but perfect, and by no means too snobbishly prepared, farmer's food. Their carbonara was delicious, a recipe that opened a new door to the world of pasta for the hundreds of thousands who bought the restaurant's groundbreaking blue cookbook. And it's a good recipe, although controversial; in some circles it's even considered heretical, because instead of guanciale it contains pancetta, and parmesan instead of pecorino. But most importantly, and possibly the worst thing of all: it contains cream. It tastes good, but it's not how it should be. The River Café took most of its recipes from Tuscany, and the rest from northern Italy. So their delicious carbonara —any Roman will argue—isn't correct. It isn't authentic.

It's easy to overstate how concerned Italians are with food. And it's certainly not true that they all are. On my first visit to Rome, I was obsessed with eating "where the locals ate." I was quite thorough about it and followed a stream of office clerks heading to lunch at a randomly picked spot on the outskirts of town, some distance from the main tourist attractions. I walked away from a nice trattoria at a roundabout after seeing that their menu was in Italian and English, but was content when I found myself, as the only foreigner, in a sparsely furnished room with fluorescent lighting and an authentically complicated ordering system.

But hold on, what's this? My shock at being served a soggy cloth of a pizza was magnified by a characteristic "ping" from the kitchen, the chiming bell hailing the microwave oven's triumph of convenience. But? I was surrounded by Italians! The people who had decided to eat lunch here and not on the trattoria at the roundabout, it turned out, weren't doing so because it was a hidden gem but because they wanted something cheap and fast.

And it's the same everywhere. The impressive Italian supermarkets, with hundreds of different olive oils, bountiful vegetable counters, and meat counters selling whole rabbits, ducks, and piglets, have an almost equally impressive selection of ready meals, the world's largest bags of cheese puffs, luminous green soda that makes Coca-Cola look like a health drink—and packets of carbonara sauce. Many Italians prefer this, or don't know any better. But for every person who doesn't care, there are enough who make a big deal of it, protesting when something is wrong and rewarding those who stick to tradition.

At the table next to mine sits a mother with her three children, who are roughly the same age as mine, only far better behaved. The two boys and a girl sit nicely and eat, and I'm fascinated by how they don't squirm around in the seats, like my children tend to do. They don't shout, and they handle the knives and forks like useful tools which they've mastered. They are like small people, not wild animals. The whole family has ordered carbonara, and they eat it with devotion and reverence. At regular intervals, the youngest of the well-behaved children puts down his knife and fork and in a solemn voice says to everyone at the table, "La vera carbonara!"— the real carbonara—before picking up his cutlery and continuing to eat. The family, it turns out, are originally from Rome, but currently live in Abruzzo to the east. "We were on vacation in New York recently," explains the mother. "And we were served carbonara at a so-called Italian restaurant, and it was so . . . awful. It made the children cry. My youngest was particularly upset, so that's why I brought them here."

"Why do you think they make carbonara like that?" I ask.

"I have no idea," replies the mother.

"I think it's because they like to play with Italians' feelings," declares the eldest son.

Above all, Italian cuisine is about this: authenticity. French gastronomy is concerned with tradition, but also with revolution. "Today I'm going to compose a dish the world has never seen before," the French master chef Alain Passard says to himself before going to work each day. In France, people don't hesitate to call their top chefs artists; they almost demand that chefs surprise and shock and lead them into a wonderland of novelty. Italian chefs do not pretend to have invented anything. They profess to have roots in ancient and better times. *La cucina autentica* is *la cucina di nonna*—Grandma's kitchen. And Grandma's kitchen should be unaffected by food trends and external influences. "Only by living in Italy, by knowing its traditions and being in constant contact with its day-to-day life, is it possible to understand, evaluate, and select the dishes that constitute true home cooking," writes Paolo Petrini in his preface to the academy's culinary bible, *La Cucina*, a collection of "more than 2,000 authentic recipes from all over Italy."

Italian food is probably the world's most successful. You will find pizza, pasta, balsamic vinegar, and parmesan all over the world. But what makes Italian food extra successful is that—in addition to becoming readily available—it has preserved its soul. It's almost as if, through the food, you can hear the people of Italy saying: "You can visit, and buy our food and our wine, and experience our hospitality, but you cannot buy us or influence our culture with your taste." Italians live off the world buying their food, and the country being one of the most touristy there is. But they continue to insist on it being done correctly—Grandma's way. I'm probably not the only person to have seen a waiter rushing to prevent what he considers a clear and present danger, seeing a guest about to sprinkle parmesan onto a seafood pasta. And non-Italians continue to buy the academy's huge cookbook in the hope of making genuine Italian food, despite its preface stating that it's quite impossible.

The carbonara I make is pretty good. I definitely spend more time on it, and I'm certainly more generous with the ingredients than they are at La Carbonara, but whenever I eat it there, I still think it's much better than my own. Even after buying everything I need from Italy, it's still not as good. At La Carbonara it's authentic. *La cucina autentica* is one of the reasons Italian food often drives me crazy. It's so rigid! So laborious! So insistent on being excellent! But at the same time, it's also the reason I never get bored of it. I'm constantly being reminded of what makes Italian cuisine so beautiful, so sophisticated in all its simplicity. It's about the little, important things, like how chef Valentina only uses capers from Salina in her rabbit stew; the way she moves her hands when rinsing them in water before use; and the extra work needed to create the rich flavor of a tomato sauce that can only contain tomato, garlic, olive oil, and basil. Making the perfect carbonara requires a musicality that makes me think that Petrini could be right, that you do have to be Italian and live in Italy to succeed.

But just how genuine *is* all this? Was carbonara—today one of the most important Roman dishes—invented by the coal seller's wife Domenica, the grandmother of Maria the restaurant's current owner, or by a collective of coal merchants, as history would have it? When I asked Maria's husband, Dario Martelli, he dismissed it outright. "Invented pasta carbonara? It's like asking who invented beds," he replied. The dish, as he saw it, was a kind of platonic idea, an eternal part of Italy's culinary DNA. It sounds right, in a way, compatible with the concept of Italian food being like an ancient tree with various branches.

The problem is, there's no mention of the dish in any old cookbooks. For example, it's not mentioned in the biggest and most important book about Roman cuisine, Ada Boni's recipe collection from 1930. So where did it come from? And how did it become so important that it was worth dumping your boyfriend over, or writing manifestos to protect it?

Another account of carbonara's origins goes like this: When Rome was liberated by Allied troops in 1944, the city was in fairly good shape compared to other war-ravaged cities at the time. There had been some bombing in 1943, but since the city was home to the Vatican—and no one wanted to be responsible for destroying important historic monuments, let alone do something that could be seen as an attack on the Catholic Church's supreme spiritual leader and a city considered holy or at least very important by all of Christianity—Rome had escaped without major destruction or loss of life. Italy was, nevertheless, in a state of emergency. The entire nation was poverty-stricken after years of war, and in Rome—which had always been dependent on a supply of provisions from outside—there was a shortage of food. On June 4, 1944, thousands of American occupying forces arrived in the city, where they were met by cheering in the streets. And these soldiers, as they did in Paris and other liberated cities, became important customers for local restaurants and cafés. They had dollars, nylon stockings, tobacco, and, not least, food from the United States' rich agricultural areas, where the fields were lush and the barns were full.

What the Americans didn't have, however, was any particular interest in Italian food, which they saw as foreign, fatty, and strange. The romanticizing of Italian food didn't begin until several decades later. For corn-fed Midwestern soldiers, Bill, Al, and Chuck, the thought of eating food containing anchovies and garlic was repulsive. Not to mention the Roman specialties, such as artichokes and offal.

This, according to food historian Alan Davidson, was quite crucial to the development of pasta carbonara. It was at precisely that time, in the years during and immediately after the war, that the dish may have originated. The soldiers' rations included rare ingredients like bacon and eggs, sometimes tinned cream. But they had no interest in cooking themselves, or eating at the army barracks. This resulted in them bringing their own ingredients to restaurants, where they had the local chefs prepare dishes less challenging to their restrictive and sensitive tastebuds. So according to this alternative origin story, the first proto-carbonara was American, or a kind of Italian–American hybrid. Italian pasta, with bacon, eggs, and cream from the Land of Plenty. But then came peace. And the moment the American soldiers left, the dish's recipe was brought into line. Any trace of its foreign origin was hidden, and carbonara became Italian—an inalienable part of its cultural heritage.

AS WE SIT in the restaurant—several well-dressed people and their well-mannered children, enjoying the local and regional specialties while having an enlightened conversation—it's easy to understand what the academy means by "the civilization of the table." Imagine the conversations that have taken place around these tables, and at the thousands of other restaurants in Rome and around Italy. Imagine the ideas that have taken shape, sketches that have been drawn on napkins, melodies hummed, love affairs initiated. And imagine all the food that has flowed from the kitchen and left us content and replenished. But if one looks more closely at this "civilization of the table," it's quite possible to go further than the academy does: one could even claim that "civilization of the table" and "civilization" are the same thing.

Today, it's seen as corny and old-fashioned, perhaps even racist, to talk about civilization. It is often associated with attempts to impose one type of civilization—usually the European one—on

societies that are seen as less civilized, often for random or preju-
diced reasons. "Two Zulus, slightly affected by civilization," says
the caption on a photograph in my well-meaning great-grandfather's
travelogue, "Among Blacks and Whites in South Africa," written a
hundred years ago on behalf of the Scandinavian Alliance Mission.
The two were partially dressed and therefore considered "slightly"
civilized, as opposed to the naked natives, who in the eyes of the
missionaries were uncivilized. But civilization isn't determined
by the amount of clothing one wears. The word itself comes from
Latin, *civilis,* and is associated with the organization of societies in
cities, city-states, or other concentrated clusters where the sum of
people constituted a greater whole and where various specialized
tasks were carried out.

Here in Rome, where under every ancient monument there are
even older ruins, it's easy to forget how short this part of human
history is. We need go back only 14,000 years to find all the world's
people living in nomadic groups that subsisted as hunter-gatherers.
In his book *Against the Grain,* James C. Scott talks about the archeological discoveries from early human societies that show how the
diet of one group could consist of as many as twenty different
mammals, sixteen bird families, and more than 140 different plants,
seeds, pulses, and nuts. The American anthropologist Marshall
Sahlin calls this hunter-gatherer society the "original affluent society," where most people were well fed owing to a varied diet, and
had many hours of free time every day, which could be used for
social interaction.

About 14,000 years ago, the development that would lead to
what we now know as civilization began. In the area known as
the Fertile Crescent—the no-longer-so-fertile area of present-day
Egypt, through Israel, parts of Syria, Turkey, Iraq, and Iran—several

types of grass began to spread, among them the predecessors of today's wheat—emmer and einkorn. The grass had probably always been there, but non-man-made climate change led to it suddenly having better growing conditions. Wet, mild winters and hot, dry summers gave fast-growing annual plants an advantage over perennials. At first, people must have picked the grass seeds without making much out of it; the grain would have been just an additional supplement to their 140-plant diet. But since the grain contained far more nourishment than the other crops, it became increasingly important. Why go leaping from rock to rock, hunting for sour berries and bitter leaves, when you can pick grain that provides more sustenance?

One of the drawbacks with the various wild wheats is that they don't see themselves as food. For the plant, the grains are its chance of reproducing, and the first thing it will do when they're ripe is to disperse them. When the time comes, the grain will detach from the head, ready to be blown away by a gust of wind and ensure the survival of the species. This is convenient for the plant but less so for humans, who had to compete with the birds, animals, and insects and pick it up from the ground, one grain at a time. While searching for the nutritious grains, humans found that some heads didn't release their grains after maturing. This was due to a genetic defect, something that would normally lead straight into a Darwinian cul-de-sac—but since it actually made it easier for people to harvest the wheat, the genetic defect became a criterion for success.

As humans gradually realized that they could get higher yields by looking after some of the defective grains and then scattering them in the fields, more and more of the grains remained attached to the heads. Many generations later, the grain cultivated by humans had changed from the wild variety. It no longer dropped its seeds when it matured and was dependent on humans to complete its life cycle. This story repeated itself again and again throughout the agricultural era: we humans took a naturally occurring plant or animal, which we kept captive, and manipulated it over generations to give it qualities that would benefit us.

However, grain wasn't the only thing to become tamed. As we figured out how to maximize the yield through sowing, and perhaps even watering, we invested so much in these patches of soil that it became important for us to ensure that those of us who did the sowing—not a competing group or some undeserving animal—got to harvest the crop. In other words, we had to stay nearby. We settled near the crops, and as we were no longer traveling from place to place, we started building houses.

The increase in productivity meant that more people could live in the same area. It also led to competition and conflict over resources. To defend themselves against attacks from rival groups, people started living closer together. And to insure against unexpected variations in the yield, the grain was collected in a central store. As these stores grew, someone had to look after them, and in order for the system to be fair they developed ways of noting how much each person had contributed. The grain store and the village needed protecting too. This development, as the Israeli historian Yuval Harari points out, had some clear drawbacks as well as upsides: our bodies were suited for climbing trees and hunting gazelles, not loosening rocks and carrying water buckets. Farming brought a range of new ailments with it. Harari, Scott, and a number of others point out how the transition to agriculture probably led to more diseases, shorter life expectancy, and a less varied diet. But it also gave us something new: for the first time, we had a surplus of food.

We are, of course, racing through thousands of years of history here. There is heated debate among historians, archeologists, and biologists about how, and how quickly, these changes occurred; or whether the introduction of agriculture was a step forward or "our biggest mistake," as the American geographer and biologist Jared Diamond puts it. Or perhaps they were, as I believe, a prerequisite for many of our joys and troubles, all the things that hundreds of generations later have given us eyestrain and ice cream, telesales and craft ales, fake news and fireworks, pandemics and pasta—just about everything we love and hate.

In any case, there seems to be agreement on the main points: grain was the reason we settled in one place and organized ourselves into larger settlements; why we developed organized religion and written language; and what brought us ruling classes, laws and taxes, priests, warriors, and professions that didn't even contribute to the production of food.

We domesticated grain. But equally important, as Harari points out, was that grain domesticated and civilized us. In this sense, all civilization is, in reality, "the civilization of the table."

PEPPER

In the science-fiction film *Demolition Man*, the policeman John Spartan wakes up in the future after being cryogenically frozen for decades. He encounters an almost unrecognizable society, a high-tech dystopia where people eat recycled food—"Great for the environment and OK for you"—and you have to use shells, not toilet paper, when visiting the bathroom. A time traveler from the Roman era visiting the present day would probably feel even more alienated. Telephones, electricity, and the Internet would seem incomprehensible, and the absence of slaves would strike him as weird and impractical. Most of our food would also be quite unrecognizable. Of what's now taken for granted as being part of Italy and Rome's timeless cuisine, a large part has come about more recently. The ancient Romans didn't have pasta, pizza, coffee, or rice—and tiramisu was 2,000 years away. The time-traveling Roman would be baffled by forks, and look both amazed and skeptically at the sight of tomatoes, aubergines, peppers, and potatoes.

The restaurant La Campana, a few blocks further north of Campo de' Fiori, near Rione Ponte—the site of La Carbonara's first, modest coal-merchant-and-restaurant—boasts of being Rome's oldest restaurant. It recently celebrated its five-hundredth anniversary; half a millennium of continuous—or almost continuous—business. The modest-looking eatery in a narrow alleyway—or *vicolo*—is frequented by members of society's upper echelons: writers, businessmen, and politicians. The former president, Napolitano, was a regular here, as was Federico Fellini, and—if we're to believe the restaurant's marketing—Goethe and Caravaggio in their time. A majority of the dishes on the menu are similar to those found at other Roman restaurants; an assortment of popular, not especially modern, although not particularly old dishes. There are boiled and fried vegetables for antipasto, and the most common pasta dishes for *primi*, among them *fettucine Alfredo*, which could well be the world's most boring pasta dish. *Fettucine Alfredo* contains only pasta, butter, cream, and parmesan; it is a pale and somewhat tasteless relative of carbonara. The dish is a kind of local specialty in that it was supposedly invented at the neighboring restaurant, Alfredo alla Scrofa, in honor of the silent film stars Douglas Fairbanks and Mary Pickford on their honeymoon in 1920. Like the American soldiers during the Second World War, they were suspicious of strange and unusual flavors. As a *secondi*, La Campana offers simple and hearty meat dishes. Had it not been for the restaurant's five-hundred-year history—which you're constantly reminded of by the inscription on its logo, "Il ristorante più antico di Roma"—you might think this was any of the city's classic restaurants.

However, La Campana's signature dish, *vignarola di verdure*, a stew consisting of broad beans, pancetta, and peas, has remained virtually unchanged since the restaurant first opened. "It could have been served five hundred years ago. Or two thousand years ago," claimed the owner Paolo Trancassini when I ate there during my last visit to Rome. "We have never done anything to the dish, nor would we ever consider modernizing it." In general, there's good reason to be wary of the stories restaurant owners use as selling points. As well as being a restaurateur and a distant relative of the family running La Carbonara, Trancassini is also a politician in the post-post-fascist Fratelli d'Italia party. In this sense he has a political motive for portraying himself as a steward of traditions and eternal Roman values. Yet their *vignarola di verdure* is so simple, and the components so fundamental, that it's quite possible that the recipe is exactly as it was during Roman times. It consists of old-fashioned vegetables, boiled together in a slow, old-fashioned way that makes them lose their color and turn brownish-green, but also makes them taste more like themselves.

Another thing a visitor from the Roman era would notice is the offal. Today's Romans have retained their love of what they call the "fifth quarter" of the beast. Most Roman restaurants serve *trippa* (tripe). These animal stomachs are still displayed in restaurant windows, where they lie, looking a bit like a collection of old bathing caps, not the condom-like ones that today's Olympic swimmers use, but ruffled, like the one my grandmother wore at the municipal pool. At Checchino dal 1887, a restaurant in Testaccio in southern Rome close to the old city walls, offal is almost the only thing on the menu. To say that there is history in its walls is an understatement: the restaurant is dug into Monte Testaccio, the mountain of shattered olive oil pots from the Roman era. In addition to classics like *trippa*, they serve a number of other offal-based specialties, such as pig's trotters, oxtail, *pajata*, tongue, liver, brain, sweetbread, and testicles. My initial thought when I looked at their menu the first time I visited was that testicles must be one of the most shocking things you can serve. But that was before someone told me what *pajata* was.

Pajata are unwashed calf intestines full of what was in the intestine when the calf was slaughtered. We are, it must be noted, not talking about just any calf, but a young animal that still only drinks milk. The milk, which is partially digested, goes through a kind of natural cheese-making process within the intestine, helped by the enzymes in the calf's stomach. The dish is shockingly out of step with modern ethics and aesthetics: unwashed intestines! From calves still drinking their mother's milk! But that was the kind of food the classical Romans loved. And they didn't stop there: in Roman times udder was considered a delicacy, and they would occasionally eat placenta as well.

I had to overcome a degree of skepticism before tucking into the intestines, but I was surprised at how mild and pleasant they tasted. I was dreading the bilious taste you can sometimes get from stomach, which means I normally stay well away from *trippa* if possible. But the *pajata* actually tasted fresh, almost like cream cheese or freshly made ricotta. At the same time, I also had the most distinct feeling that I was eating a food of the past, something archaic that will probably never be anything more than a historical curiosity. Today, grandparents take their grandchildren to Checchino dal 1887 to show them what kind of food their *own* grandparents used to eat. Unfortunately, it's a tradition fewer and fewer people are continuing, according to the restaurant's owner, Francesco Mariani, who after the meal took me into the kitchen to meet his brother, the chef. While I was back there he also showed me the wine cellar, where a cool wind blows through the 2,000-year-old pot shards and the floor crunches beneath your feet. Francesco's son is taking over the restaurant. He wants to start a nightclub and has already applied to rebuild parts of the premises.

Good Roman families pride themselves on having unbroken lineages without a drop of peasant blood in their veins. Similarly, it should be possible to trace today's Roman dishes so far back that you end up lost in a very, very distant past. It is an illusion, of course, since many of the "timeless classics" are relatively modern constructions. If the "American hypothesis" is true—that pasta carbonara was invented just after the Second World War—then carbonara is actually younger than the reviled fascist monumentalism blighting the eternal city. While attempting to recreate the greatness of Roman times, Mussolini and his architects committed the most fundamental of errors, an unforgivable Roman sin: they built things that were irrefutably and demonstratively new.

Our time-traveling Roman, sitting there on a flimsy modern restaurant chair—with no way of lying down to eat, as he was accustomed—would recognize the oil and the bread on the table before him. The wine would taste stronger to him, more concentrated and less musty than the wine he was used to. He would have probably diluted it with water and then nodded in recognition. "There! That's how it should be." And although the creamy pasta dish would have seemed contrary to his understanding of how food should be, our time traveler would at the very least have recognized the warm sting of pepper, one of the central, timeless flavors of Rome—the most important, perhaps. In Tuscany, fennel is the defining flavor, the one that makes you think: "Ah, Tuscany!" In Genoa it is basil. In Sardinia, they have *bottarga*—cured fish roe. Outside Naples, they are rightly proud of their tomatoes, so much so that they have tomatoes in almost every dish. In Rome, it's pepper. Pepper is an important part of *cacio pepe* (pasta with pepper and cheese) as well as carbonara; it's used as tiny burning surprises in their cured sausages, and in anything else requiring a little more fire.

I'm already tucking into my own pasta carbonara when I notice that there's not enough pepper in it. I respect orthodoxy and I'm sure they haven't just forgotten, but I still think the dish is best served with a little more pepper than they use at La Carbonara this time. I wave to Angelo. On my third try, I catch his attention. Solemnly, or perhaps a little annoyed, or just stressed because the restaurant is at its busiest, Angelo grinds pepper over my half-eaten pasta. One, two, three rounds. Then he puts down the pepper mill and rushes off. The bite from the pepper gives the carbonara a little more kick. It always surprises me how these tiny black specks have so much power to transform food: from pasta smothered in a rich sauce, to pasta carbonara—the world's greatest dish.

A dish can sometimes have its own liturgy, which has to be followed to the very last detail—it can be the order in which the ingredients have to be added, the types of olives that should be used in the different stews, the way you stir the butter and parmesan into a risotto—or just how you add that little dash of pepper to a pasta carbonara. The pepper makes the taste of guanciale more distinct, and is like the lively bubbles in a champagne to the creamy mixture of eggs and cheese. Pepper is carbonara's holy spirit.

The taste of pepper is also the taste of something greater. Pepper is the big wide world, money, and civilization. While chilis, tomatoes, and the other American foods are well-assimilated immigrants that grow quite naturally in Italy, pepper has always come from some far-flung place, over the hills and far away. Nobody has ever managed to grow pepper in or near the city. Nor anywhere else in the Roman Empire for that matter, even when the empire was at its greatest. Nevertheless, it was pepper that became the flavor of Rome.

In the second century BC, the statesman and author Cato the Elder published a book on agriculture, *De agri cultura*, which contains what are considered to be some of the oldest written recipes, including a recipe for *epityrum*, an early version of the puréed olive dish we now know as tapenade. Cato also had a recipe for a kind of cheesecake consisting of multiple layers of dough and cream cheese topped with honey. In Cato's time, the ideal was for city dwellers to be familiar with rural life, to live simply and modestly, and be wary of the corrupting effects of trade and money. And the food had to be rustic—country-style.

Two hundred years later, the situation had changed completely. The empire had replaced the republic, excessive indulgence was commonplace, and the emperors had started going bonkers. Caligula appointed his horse as senator. Nero killed his mother, then his half-brother, and then his wife. He would no doubt have been remembered for being the first head of state to enter into a gay marriage—and it was he who dressed as the bride—had he not upstaged himself by getting, somewhat unfairly, known for setting Rome alight and playing the lyre while the city burned. It was during this time and in these far from ascetic surroundings that the book often regarded as the world's first cookbook was published. *De re coquinaria* or *Apicius* is tangible proof that the Romans did not want to live like country folk. They did not want to grow their own food and loved the idea of getting luxurious produce from all around the world. The book, which is actually a collection of ten manuscripts, is often credited to Marcus Gavius Apicius, although it's doubtful whether he wrote it himself.

Apicius was a man of his time who truly embraced the values of the empire, not least its excesses. Among food lovers, he is considered a slightly tragic hero, a wealthy and pleasure-seeking *bon vivant* who would eat flamingo tongues and the fatty liver from force-fed geese, what we today call foie gras. He even developed a way of fattening pigs to make their livers oversized, and would then kill them by drowning them in—or letting them drink themselves to death with—*mulsum*, wine with honey added to it.

On one occasion, Apicius heard that the shrimp on the other side of the Mediterranean were bigger and better than those found further north—perhaps the best in the world it was claimed. For him, not having access to this delicacy was unbearable, and it became an obsession. He just had to have them, and decided quite simply to emigrate. No point living here in this tiny-shrimped place! Apicius loaded his belongings onto two ships and headed south, where his escort ran into a group of Libyan fishing boats just off the coast. It turned out that the shrimp in the Libyan waters were no bigger or better than at home. So he turned his ships around and sailed back again without setting a foot on land.

Today's gastro-tourists are often criticized for their level of consumption, for traveling to Copenhagen, Lima, and Bangkok in search of new flavors. But although their journeys are often longer, they can't match the dedication and resources Apicius put into his quest to find the world's best shrimp. As could be suspected, Apicius' playboy lifestyle wasn't sustainable in the long run. When he had finally spent all his money on food and fun, he killed himself. Better to do that than cut the domestic budget. *De re coquinaria* is often simply referred to as *Apicius*, and is one of the leading sources of information about Roman cooking. The collection describes the procedures for almost everything a rich household could need in order to stay fat and content, from pickling and juicing, to recipes for party food and—for those who really, really like eating, and want to eat even more—laxatives, to speed up your bowel movements.

One of my favorite recipes is one that's presented as an "every-day dish"—*patina quotidiana*. Consisting of boiled fish, chicken, pepper, sweet wine, eggs, and sorrel, it requires a particular Roman pantry and an equally unusual Roman palate to appreciate the strange combination of flavors. The choice of ingredients in *Apicius* indicates that there was an extensive trade of goods from remote parts of the world, and an insatiable demand for things that were exotic and exclusive. There are recipes for flamingo, pigeon, crane, pheasant, and ostrich, not to mention truffles, suckling pig, gazelles, oysters, rays, sea urchins, and dormice, small rodents that look like a cross between a squirrel and a shrew.

Common to many of these dishes is that they include *garum*, the Romans' universal sauce made out of fermented fish guts, not too dissimilar to Thai fish sauce. And at the centre of all this is pepper, which was used in almost everything. Pepper added a little edge to spicy wine, sausages, shellfish sauce, brain pudding, scallops, pumpkin, lettuce, desserts, and fish quenelles. It's hard to keep count, but when I run a search in Project Gutenberg's electronic translation of *Apicius*, the word "pepper" is mentioned 468 times. By comparison, garlic is mentioned four times. That is not to say that pepper was more common than garlic among the population as a whole; Apicius' world was that of the upper classes. You could perhaps say that pepper was the upper-class garlic—something that was always included, a preferred taste and a marker of status.

Exotic spices began appearing in Europe around 500 BC, and the first sources we have about them being there come from the Greek city-states. Spices offered flavors and smells that bore no resemblance to anything we'd experienced in nature. And this mysteriousness gave them an extra dimension.

What were they? At first it was believed that spices didn't really come from Earth but were fragments of paradise, tiny flecks from the world of the gods. Guinea pepper, long one of several competing pepper varieties (and not related to real pepper), still goes by the name "grains of paradise" in English, and variants of "paradise seeds" in several other languages.

Why spices? If you've holidayed along the Mediterranean and hiked through landscapes that smell of thyme and oregano, you'll know that there's no shortage of aromatic plants that can be used for cooking. It's easy to think that Greek or Italian food could have done just fine without exotic spices. A leg of lamb with garlic, herbs, and olives doesn't necessarily get better if it's accompanied by pepper, cinnamon, or cloves. But they impart a taste of a wider world, and it's hard to overestimate how much the arrival of spices greatly affected our worldview, psychology, and gastronomy.

A person living in Greece 2,500 years ago, or during the Roman Empire 2,000 years ago, would have known that something else lay beyond the countryside, city, or valley. Both rural farms and urban houses were manned by slaves who came from recently conquered areas, and when Rome had won important battles far away triumphal processions would be held where plundered valuables, exotic animals, slaves, and other spoils of war were displayed. Scholars generally understood that it was cold in the north, while it was hot and mostly dry in the south on the other side of the Mediterranean. But they knew very little about the world beyond the empire's borders. Maps were scarce, and those they did have faded into white environs, or were full of mythical beasts and deities at the edges.

Pepper and other exotic spices were like postcards from another world, fragrant proof that there actually was something out there. Imagine holding a peppercorn or a piece of cinnamon for the first time! Just as Copernicus's and Bruno's theories laid the foundation for a new way of thinking, where humans had to look at themselves differently, as part of a universe, pepper was a seed that planted the idea of the Earth they inhabited being a bigger place. While salt was the first regular commodity, a connector of different regions, a necessity, pepper was the first global commodity – a luxury of great cultural importance. Pepper made the world expand.

Those two or three rounds with a pepper grinder are still a small miracle. After being picked, dried, stored, and transported, and then left for weeks, months, or even years in grocery stores or kitchen cupboards, just one slight movement can release the flavor sealed within and make it explode. Salt brings out a food's basic flavor, but pepper gives it its kick.

Two thousand years ago, the spice trade was already extensive. Spices were sold to local traders, first at their place of origin in India, later from other eastern locations; they then make a long journey, changing hands numerous times along the way—and with each exchange the price would increase significantly. Customs fees or protection money would be demanded, and the various traders would also have to make a profit. Tons upon tons were transported from India and sold to Roman, Greek, and later other European elites. It was dangerous, laborious, and lucrative.

Since the trade routes bringing the spices west were long and involved many different traders, the spices' origins were often unclear, even to the merchants themselves. If you were responsible for a stretch of what is now Jordan, you perhaps knew that your spices had come from traders who'd bought them from some other traders from Mecca, such as the Prophet Muhammad's wife's powerful family. But where *they* had actually acquired them would have been a mystery to you. The traders had a vested interest in protecting their spice sources from their customers and other traders. Nothing comes from nowhere, so stories about the origins of these spices would appear, each more fantastic than the last—to satisfy people's curiosity and help justify the high prices.

One of the most important early sources about the spice trade is the Greek historian Herodotus, who lived in the fifth century BC and has been called the "Father of History." His book *The Histories* is a wonderful mix of accounts of historical events, stories about different peoples, and descriptions of geographical and natural phenomena; the science of the era is punctuated by what can best be called rumors and prejudices. The book is so full of phenomenal stories, of such questionable veracity, that Herodotus has also been called the "Father of Lies." About cinnamon (or true cinnamon) and its slightly coarser relative cinnamon cassia—which are nowadays sold as one and the same thing—he writes the following:

> the Arabians . . . cover all their body and their face with the hides of oxen and other skins, leaving only holes for the eyes, and thus protected go in search of the cassia, which grows in a lake of no great depth. All round the shores and in the lake itself there dwell a number of winged animals, much resembling bats, which screech horribly, and are very valiant. These creatures they must keep from their eyes all the while that they gather the cassia. Still more wonderful is the mode in which they collect the cinnamon. Where the wood grows, and what country produces it, they cannot tell . . . only some, following probability, relate that it comes from the country in which Bacchus was brought up. Great birds, they say, bring the sticks which we Greeks, taking the word from the Phoenicians, call cinnamon, and carry them up into the air to make their nests. These are fastened with a sort of mud to a sheer face of rock, where no foot of man is able to climb. So the Arabians, to get the cinnamon, use the following artifice. They cut all the oxen and asses and beasts of burden that die in their land into large pieces, which they carry with them into those regions, and place near the nests; then they withdraw to a distance, and the old birds, swooping down, seize the pieces of meat and fly with them up to their nests; which, not being able to support

the weight, break off and fall to the ground. Hereupon the Arabians return and collect the cinnamon, which is afterward carried from Arabia into other countries.

Along with pepper, cinnamon cassia and true cinnamon were among the first spices to became the objects of an intercontinental spice trade. Of course, there were those who suspected that Herodotus' stories were themselves spiced with a liberal amount of imagination and travelers' tales. Five hundred years later, these myths were sniffed out by Herodotus' Roman colleague Pliny the Elder, who—with fairly good reason—claimed they were the invention of Arab traders wanting to inflate the prices of their goods. Any sensible person could understand that the terrible bats and enormous birds were pure fantasy, he argued. In order to set the record straight, he explained that cinnamon was in fact from Ethiopia. It was purchased inland and transported first to the coast and then across the sea in primitive rafts without rudders or sails, a journey that took five years and cost many human lives, before the cinnamon finally ended up in the port of Yemen, where it was bought by Arabs.

With even the myth-busting soothsayer spouting nonsense, it must have been hard to know what to believe. It's true that the spice passed through the port of Yemen, but it was virtually the only thing Pliny's version of the story got right. Knowledge of where the spices originated came in waves that washed up as much nonsense as they did facts. It was also quite normal for the old, more-or-less true stories to be replaced with newer, taller ones. And these fanciful tales persisted, even as we were simultaneously learning more about the world, because neither historians nor traders wanted to sacrifice their profitable stories on the altar of truth.

The real story of cinnamon and cassia is a bit of a disappointment, at least compared to the stories people were told. Both come from the dried bark of trees that are neither rare nor particularly difficult to grow. But the smell and taste are both fantastic—two qualities that demanded a high price if supplies were limited and the stories about its origins were adventurous enough.

A thousand years later, European scholars had a reasonably precise idea about the origins of the various spices. Cinnamon came from Sri Lanka; the slightly coarser cassia was from further east, Indonesia and China. Pepper came from South India. But there were still mythical creatures dwelling at the edge of the map, just as there were stories about the value and almost magical effects of spices.

Black pepper is the unripened berry of a vine that originates from the mountainous areas of southern India. In some places it is still farmed in much the same way as it would have been 2,000 years ago. Since the plant cannot manage on its own and needs to be supported, it is often grown between other shrubs or trees for it to climb. In the state of Kerala, where pepper comes from and where they grow what's often considered the best pepper, most people continue to do so on a small scale. When I traveled there in connection with a book I wrote about spices in the early 2000s, my plan was to visit a pepper plantation. I traveled to the mountains where pepper has been grown since the dawn of time, but I couldn't find any plantations. The average pepper farmer, it turned out, grows only a few pounds a year, enough for a little extra income besides their simple self-sufficient farm.

The berries ripen in several waves throughout the year, so harvesting is an almost continuous affair, with the mother and father constantly moving around the little garden, up on their ladders, searching for pepper berries that are at the right level of maturity. When one round of the garden has been completed, the next round has to begin. Outside the houses I visited, there were carpets of freshly picked berries laid out to dry. These small-scale farmers are vulnerable to fraud by greedy buyers, so to protect them Kerala's communist government have used the tools of the market economy to set up the International Pepper Exchange, where the prices of pepper are determined through buying and selling. These prices are read out on the radio every night to keep the farmers informed of the current rate.

One thing that struck me while I was out on the pepper farms was how I didn't see any black pepper on the vines. The farmers picked the berries when they were at their largest, but still green. While the pepper berries are slowly drying on mats or grates—a process that's the same on a large plantation as it is on a small farm in Kerala—a natural fermentation process occurs under its skin. At this point the berry's color changes from green to black, and its flavor is transformed from green and grassy to the complex, aromatic taste of black pepper. The green peppercorns you buy in the store are really the same peppercorns, except that their maturation has been stopped, usually by treating them with a chemical. White pepper is made from berries that were picked when ripe and that have had their skin removed.

In the port city of Cochin, too, most things were more or less as they must have been 2,000 years ago. Except for the Pepper Exchange, where a group of heavy-eyed traders monitored the pepper prices on computer screens, all the processes were slow and manual. It is here that the sacks are opened and the peppercorns sorted and graded. To get into one of the sorting houses, I had to take off my shoes and climb over the six-foot-high mountains of peppercorns that tickled the soles of my feet. Inside, where the air was thick with pepper dust, men and women sat sorting the peppercorns by hand, one at a time. I noticed that the shriveled husks which fell from the damaged white or black peppercorns were also kept; no doubt to be used as the basis of the small bags of pepper you get with airplane food, which taste more like dust than spice.

Most of us learn two things about the history and origins of pepper: the first is that pepper was once as expensive as gold. The second is that pepper and other spices were used to mask the flavor of meat or any other food that had gone rotten. What is certain, and can be ascertained just by logic, without checking any historical prices or old cookbooks, is that both claims cannot be true. If spices had been that valuable—perhaps almost as valuable as gold—it wouldn't make sense for them to be used on something as trivial as meat, let alone bad meat. You wouldn't use gold to repair a broken shoe, or champagne to make sour milk taste better. It was surely cheaper to buy new meat than to try and rescue old meat with valuable pepper, if it cost as much as gold. Besides, it doesn't help. Nothing, not even pepper, chili, or liquor, can make rotten meat taste good.

But just how expensive were peppers and spices really? Spice prices must have varied according to supply and demand and any conflicts or troubles along the trade routes, just as oil and other commodity prices vary today. Of course the simplest way of putting it is to just say that spices were expensive. At the same time, terms like "expensive" and "cheap" meant something completely different 2,000 years ago. The vast majority of people were so poor that they lived hand-to-mouth, either on meagre subsistence farms in the countryside or by depending on charity and food in the cities. Today we can balk at the price difference between an organic chicken and a mass-produced broiler, or a regular and craft beer, but in Roman times the food price hierarchy had many more levels.

Grain and cabbage were at the bottom of this hierarchy, cheap, sometimes free—for much of the Roman Empire's history the poor inhabitants of Rome were entitled to a certain amount of free or subsidized grain or bread. A notch more expensive, but still fairly cheap, were legumes. A few lucky places had access to large amounts of cheap fish, such as herring. Eggs and dairy products were a rare luxury for the poor who lived in the cities. Meat and fish were generally scarce, but there was a big difference between cheap offal, old chicken, or goat, and the finest cuts of veal, prime lamb, or capon. Further up were high-status meats such as goose, peacock, and swan. And at the very top, and most expensive of all, were rare animals from foreign countries and distinctly high-status commodities like flamingo tongues, which must have required huge resources to produce in any significant quantity.

Spices were also near the top of the list, but since you don't need a lot of cloves or pepper to give food a distinct character, it's almost impossible to say whether they were seen as more expensive than peacock, or less expensive than flamingo. They were certainly beyond the reach of poor and ordinary Romans. But the idea of spices being anywhere near as valuable as gold was—as I'll now try and show—a myth. Spices were exotic and rare and could be used as a means of exchange, a bit like precious metals. But they weren't gold.

One of my favorite examples of spice prices being exaggerated comes from the talented author Charles Corn in his otherwise informative book *The Scents of Eden* from 1998: "A conservative estimate is that they [the spices] rose in value one hundred percent each time they changed hands, and that this route required them to change hands hundreds of times," he writes. It seems like a fair statement—100 percent, a hundred times or more—as a rough summary of what must have undoubtedly been a long and dangerous journey from the spice's place of origin to market. Until you actually try calculating it, because if you take the number one, and increase it by 100 percent, you get two, and if you increase that by 100 percent, you get four. If you do it a hundred times, the price will have increased 633,825,300,114,114,700,748,351,602,688 times since you began. I don't even know how to say the number. Corn has unwittingly created some kind of parallel to Ibn Khallikan's story about the inventor of the chessboard who was asked what he wanted in return and replied that he just wanted one grain of rice for the first square, two for the second and so on. A seemingly moderate wish, but in reality it was more rice than in the whole of India. Had Charles Corn's account been correct, not even all the world's gold would have bought you a single peppercorn. Had he said the price increased by a hundredfold, he may have been closer to the truth, although I'm not sure that would have been "a conservative estimate" either.

We do know the price of pepper: there are numerous written sources documenting what it cost. The most famous, stated by Pliny the Elder in his *Natural History* from the second half of the first century AD, corresponds with other estimates from the time. Pliny, he who told the more-than-a-little-bit-absurd story about cinnamon, was a Roman statesman and intellectual who had tremendous creative power. His fifty volumes of historical work are lost, but his *Natural History*, comprising 37 volumes, has been saved and is an important source of knowledge about how the world looked and, not least, how his contemporaries saw the world. Pliny was among those who perished in the famous volcanic eruption of Mount Vesuvius in AD 79; not because he was unlucky enough to be in Pompeii or Herculaneum, but because he traveled into the eruption zone out of sheer curiosity, to investigate the fascinating phenomenon. The price of black pepper, stated by Pliny, was 4 denarii per Roman pound (about 11½ oz)—about 12 denarii per kilogram (2.2 lb). The denarius was a silver coin that originally weighed almost 7 grams, but was gradually made thinner. In Pliny's time, it weighed about 3.5 grams, which puts the price of pepper at 42 grams of silver per kilo, about ⅔ ounces of silver for a pound of pepper. Gold was worth around ten times as much. The point—which all the hearsay and mathematical errors obscure—is simply that spices were prohibitively expensive for ordinary people, and costly enough to represent a true expense even in households wealthy enough to afford such luxuries. Those who used pepper were like those who drink champagne and eat caviar today. And by that I don't mean supermarket champagne, but vintage champagne that comes in beautiful wooden boxes and promises to make the moment sparkle.

I have my own hypothesis about why the absurd calculations and gossip endured for so long: historians and writers will have seen spices regularly brought up in historical accounts, mentioned not only in cookbooks like *Apicius*, but in what are considered more prestigious stories, about conquests and state affairs. Based on this, historians seem to have struggled to understand why pepper and other spices became so important. "Spices must have had a function beyond what we know and use them for today," they must have thought, "more than just something to have in your food." To explain the enormous importance of spices during long periods of history, they exaggerated the prices and emphasized their role as status symbols and medicine, or even miracle cure.

The craving for exotic spices during antiquity had its critics. Emperor Augustus' daughter Julia, for example, was sent into exile after a string of scandalous and publicly known sexual escapades; it was constantly said that she had "a weakness for pepper," as though it could explain her sexual appetite. Pliny himself was negative towards the use of spices in his own time. "Why do we like pepper so much?" he asks in *Natural History*. He was amazed that we could become so fond of something that was not only expensive, but, in his opinion, not particularly easy to like. Other foods have become popular due to their sweet taste or attractive appearance, he wrote, but pepper has no such qualities: it is a flavoring, something that whets your appetite.

> Pepper has nothing to recommend it in either fruit or berry. To think that its only pleasing quality is pungency and that we go all the way to India to get this! Who was the first person who was willing to try it on his viands, or in his greed for an appetite was not content merely to be hungry? Both pepper and ginger grow wild in their own countries, and nevertheless they are bought by weight like gold or silver.

Pliny has no answers to his valid questions, but he does correctly identify where the reason for spice's success is located: in the mouth and at the table. Pepper is of course quite useless. It contains no vitamins or nutrients. It even lacks salt's ability to transform and preserve. Nonetheless, I am convinced that pepper was popular for the same reason it is today: because it tastes good, because we like it, and because sensory experiences have always been a central part of our lives.

Among Pliny's slightly cantankerous critique of meaningless pepper consumption, we also find what, as far as I know, is the first example of spice being compared to silver and gold. This is clearly meant rhetorically, to emphasize a point: pepper and ginger are just plants, so why do we make such a big deal out of them? Pliny knew well what the price of pepper was, 4 denarii, but the comparison stuck, and it persists to this day. By mentioning gold and pepper in the same sentence, he initiated a 2,000-year-long misconception that pepper fetched the same price as gold.

When Alaric the First, king of the Visigoths, stood at the gates of Rome in AD 408, the city and the Roman Empire had long been in decline. Alaric surrounded the city, and his demands for not taking it were clear: he wanted gold and silver, naturally, but also 3,000 pounds of pepper. His demands terrified the Roman traders. "What will we be left with if we give in to your demands?" they asked. "Life," replied Alaric, who also demanded 300 pounds of pepper in annual taxes. But what was life in Rome worth without gold, silver, and pepper? Without wealth, or greatness and something spicy? Without pepper, the food in Rome became no different to the food anywhere else: it lost its hallmark, and so, one could fear, would the Romans themselves. What had been a period of slow decline now accelerated. In the years that followed, Rome was subjected to a wave of looting; valuable statues were melted down and decorations torn from the buildings. The city became a shadow of its former self, and Europe entered what some have called the "Dark Ages." The apparatus of the Roman state broke down; the different peoples of its vast empire, long held together by a combination of fear and merchandise, were divided up. Its written language began to disappear. And in some parts of Europe it would be centuries before pepper returned to tables.

The spice trade didn't regain its momentum until the tenth century, and the driving force this time was Venice. This relatively small merchant city-state on the Adriatic was a major power at sea. It controlled several of the most important trade routes, and so had a monopoly on the import of spices and a range of other goods to Western Europe. Anyone who tried parallel importing would be decisively and brutally suppressed. Spices were brought by the monsoon winds from India and their other places of origin in the East across the Indian Ocean and along the Red Sea to Sinai. Only the relatively short stretch from the Red Sea to the Mediterranean took place over land. From being a preserve of the super-elite, there was now enough pepper for a larger part of the upper classes in Europe, large landholders, wealthy clergy and urban traders, to become spice consumers—a role they embraced hungrily.

The profits of all this were fantastic, and Venice's wealth was to a large degree based on its import monopoly. The author Alexandre Dumas, in addition to writing adventure novels like *The Count of Monte Cristo* and *The Three Musketeers*, wrote gastronomic literature that was almost as fantastic. In his *Grand dictionnaire de cuisine*, he writes of Venice's heyday: "The intellectual faculties [of the inhabitants] seem to have soared in an enduring exaltation under the influence of spices. Have spices given us Ariosto, Tasso, and Boccaccio? Have spices given us Titian's masterpieces? I am tempted to believe it." The money from spice trading had at least financed a great many artworks and given rich benefactors the chance to show their generosity.

The recipes from the end of the Middle Ages and the Renaissance sometimes make Apicius seem like a man of moderation, if not with flamingo tongues and his passion for shrimp, then at least when it comes to exotic spices. Absolutely everything was spiced. Cinnamon and nutmeg were common flavors, not just in cakes and desserts but in what we today consider savory foods, meat and fish dishes. Spices also spread to Europe's hinterlands. When I wrote a book about Scandinavian cooking many years ago, the oldest recipe I found was a chicken dish with saffron and cinnamon dating back to the fourteenth century. The lore of spices had reached all the way to the far corners of the world. And pepper still retained its role as the king of spices. Then came the fall of Constantinople and the Byzantine Empire, the eastern part of what remained of the Roman Empire, and the new Ottoman Empire gained control of the important trade routes to the east. Venice's monopoly had by no means been popular in the rest of Europe, but the city-state was at least part of the same European religion and cultural circles. The trade was now controlled by the same Muslims whom Europe's Christian nations had spent centuries fighting during the Crusades and religious wars. Islam, for its part, had a great deal to thank spices for. The Prophet Muhammad's first conquests were financed by his wife's earnings from the spice trade.

The peppercorn had always been a promise of another world, although one that had never been possible or necessary to travel to yourself. Now, however, the idea of finding the sea route to India went from being just a dream to a precarious need. If it could just be reached without going via the Muslim "infidels," it would end their stranglehold on the Christian world. Not to mention the enormous riches it would bring. There was a world to be conquered out there, and the peppercorn was proof.

When Christopher Columbus embarked on his perilous journey across the Atlantic in 1492, it wasn't as an explorer in search of the unknown. His goal was quite specific: to find India's pepper, spices, gold, and silk. His pledge, to return with unprecedented riches, had convinced his sponsors to fund the enterprise. Without this concrete notion of what awaited him on the other side, he would have been far less enthusiastic about going. And his pitch to the investors would have been less compelling had he been offering them a brand new continent full of things no one had heard of.

As we now know, he never made it to India. It is strange to imagine today, but when it dawned on Columbus that the continent he'd found wasn't India, he was more than a little disappointed. America was not what he'd envisioned, and it was certainly not what he'd described to his investors. For a long time he insisted that he had reached the faraway coast of India, and all the spices he found were presented as hitherto unknown relatives of pepper. Allspice, for example, was presented back home as Jamaica pepper, a name that has since gone out of fashion, but the relatives of chili and the other types of capsicum are still called a variant on the word "pepper" in Spanish, English, and a number of other languages. "There are some trees here that I think bear nutmeg," wrote Diego Álvarez Chanca, the physician and adventurer who accompanied Columbus to Hispaniola in 1494. "I say 'I believe' because the smell and taste of the bark is reminiscent of nutmeg. I saw an Indian with a ginger root round his neck." But all this was either a concoction or wishful thinking.

The other great explorer of his time was Vasco da Gama, who did what Columbus failed to achieve: he found the sea route to India, around the coast of Africa. "We are searching for spices and Christians," was his message upon reaching India in 1498. In addition to valuable spices, there were tales of lost Christian sects living on the subcontinent. The trouble was that da Gama lacked what we now call cultural sensitivity and even the most basic understanding of the continent he had arrived at. He fell to his knees before Hindu idols, believing that they represented Jesus and the Virgin Mary, and became furious after realizing his mistake.

Da Gama and his men behaved badly, even by the standards of their day. They plundered ships, fired cannons at seemingly hospitable cities, held local dignitaries captive, attempted to start a religious war with the Muslims, and strained relations with Calicut's Hindu king in ways both banal and novel. Instead of arriving with precious stones, gold, and other gifts befitting a king, as was common in all cultures at the time, they instead presented him six hats, some textiles, copper, and a modest quantity of sugar—all items that were readily available in India, and not particularly exclusive. Then they bombed Calicut. And when the relationship had soured to a thoroughly unpleasant level, da Gama aggravated things further by abducting a group of local merchants and cutting off their ears and noses, which he then sent to the king along with an insulting letter. Had da Gama only understood that this wasn't how things are done when you're visiting somewhere, the Age of Discovery might at least have gotten off to a better start.

The spice trade represented the start of several centuries of European dominance and prosperity for those countries who managed to establish themselves in the business. Central to this were the first ever multinational companies, trading enterprises that controlled world commerce. These companies went to war, conquered nations, wrote laws, and behaved like profit-driven pseudo-states free of responsibility to anyone but the shareholders in their home countries. Profits from the trading companies built cities and financed art and innovation. The new and ever-increasing wealth paved the way for an entirely different development, one that appeared to have nothing to do with spices: by plundering, deceit, military power, and divide-and-conquer tactics, a group of small

European countries ended up being like a new Roman Empire, with control over large parts of the world.

People love pleasure. Our love of everything sweet and fatty has been ingrained in us since the time when fats and readily available carbohydrates were a shortcut to survival. However, pepper, as mentioned, has no nutritional value. And its taste bears little resemblance to anything else we like. A fruit will sweeten because it wants to be eaten by animals that will disperse its seeds, thereby ensuring the spread of the species, while the aromatic oils in herbs and spices have the opposite aim: they are intended to scare. The pepper plant's potential enemies, such as insects and small rodents, are deterred by its strong taste. Humans, on the other hand, are so big that what a rodent will experience as a life-threatening attack on its senses is like a tiny pinprick. A little uncomfortable at first, but then something strange and interesting happens: the pain becomes pleasant. We're not repelled by the mild discomfort but actually find it quite enjoyable. Once we realized that pepper could be eaten without it harming us, the resistance—the brief tingle of pain—seemed worth it, like an extra challenge for our taste buds. This development, which enabled us to find pleasure in something painful and turn to strong, bitter, and sour flavors, is something we can see in our own children. The natural reaction of a baby when tasting something for the first time, whether it's a new flavor or consistency, is to pull a face and spit it out. But as any parent knows, this initial rejection won't be final, and if you try again a few seconds later, and then again and again, you'll see, after only a few attempts, something new behind the look of revulsion. Sometimes it's acceptance, sometimes curiosity. And then, after a while, pleasure and greediness. "More!"

Nature has equipped us with a sense of taste and smell that is at its sharpest when we are children. The tongue is covered by almost a million taste cells that send a constant stream of signals to the brain. It was designed to be a survival tool, specially evolved for detecting hazardous flavors before we knew which plants, seeds, and roots were wise to avoid. And that's still the case. At first, our sense of taste is acute; it's almost *too* sensitive. Every taste is intense, almost overpowering. Then, by the age of sixteen, our senses start to weaken. It happens slowly, so slowly that it's unnoticeable. And all the while this is happening we get better and better at interpreting the signals, until our taste-training is complete somewhere between the ages of 25 and 40. By then our sense of taste has been noticeably reduced. Luckily we have pepper to give us small sensory shocks.

In the early 2000s, molecular gastronomy was nearing its peak, and restaurants such as El Bulli in Catalonia and The Fat Duck outside London were vying to be the best in the world. This hyper-advanced kitchen's foremost goal was the pursuit of perfection. What was the ideal temperature for cooking a piece of meat? If 133.5°F (56.4°C) appeared to provide the right balance of tenderness and juiciness, why not just consistently cook meat at that temperature? To achieve this, special equipment was developed: the meat was wrapped in plastic and immersed in a water bath that maintained the exact temperature. Then you could just brown the meat for a few seconds to give it a nice roasted flavor. The same went for soups and sauces. Machines were built that could make them silky-soft or transform them into foam. New culinary frontiers were conquered with a combination of science and technology. And they achieved wonderful things with well-known dishes, as well. The tenderest steak. The softest sauce. Eggs that were boiled for 24 hours and had an unreal, almost jelly-like consistency. Perfection was within reach. The only problem was . . . it got boring. The first bite of the perfect steak was a revelation. It seemed impossible. Could a steak really be that tender? So juicy? The next bite was just as good, but then, with the third and fourth bite, the thrill and the pleasure became a little less intense. It was good. But was it perhaps just a bit too perfect?

To figure out what was amiss—why the perfect steak perhaps wasn't so perfect, and why people weren't excited about the soup even though it had been run through a dedicated centrifuge and the texture was more velvety than any soup hitherto known to man— the researchers connected test subjects to measuring equipment while they were eating. It turned out that the effect the food had on the test subjects would tail off. At first, the readings from their brains' sensory centers were dramatic; then, after a few bites of exactly the same thing, they ebbed away. The soup had been made according to every scientific rule, but the test subjects lost interest anyway. Even though it was perfect. Because it was perfect.

If there's anything people hate, it's monotony. We disengage and get bored. So the molecular gastronauts solved the problem by adding an imperfection, an interruption—like a crispy element in the soup, wood sorrel leaves on a purée, or what look like sherbet capsules in a velvety dessert—and they then saw a renewed level of interest. But even though research on this is relatively new, there's nothing new about the phenomenon: it is the exact reason why pepper became so popular. It attacks our taste buds, stimulates them, and makes sure we don't get bored. Pepper is the proof that we are humans, not animals, because only humans will expose themselves to a mild pain that has no other benefit than maximizing pleasure. Pepper enables us to eat a whole serving of pasta carbonara, and still be hungry for more when the plate is empty.

WINE

A high-spirited group come down the stairs from the upper-floor dining room. An elderly gentleman among them, impeccably dressed in a dark suit with a handkerchief in his breast pocket and matching tie, stumbles as he reaches the bottom, as though not expecting the final step. He tries to save himself from falling by grabbing the shoulder of a younger man in front of him, and this sets off a ripple of movement that causes another member of the party to nudge a waiter, who in turn smashes a glass. For a moment everyone's eyes are fixed on the group, while the elderly man, looking slightly abashed, is helped to his feet. Dario and Anne arrive on the scene to smooth it all over and check that everyone in the group had a successful evening. But it's impossible to mask the awkwardness that has now settled like a thick layer of silence upon the room. Everyone can see what they're not really supposed to be seeing: the old man is drunk.

Here we are, in a restaurant populated by a clientele who are nearly all drinking wine and looking condescendingly—or condemningly—at an old man who has clearly allowed himself to have one too many. Or perhaps two.

Restaurants are neutral ground. They are places to relax and have fun and do no more than pay the bill before leaving; the rest will be taken care of. And yet, you are also on show. Lack of control can be devastating. I once ate at Michelin-starred restaurant where I sat beside a family who were treating the mother to some wonderful food in luxurious surroundings, a meal where the celebrant was for once being relieved of the cooking and cleaning. The mother beamed with joy, her cheeks flushing from the wine and positive attention. But then, after visiting the toilet, she returned with a long strip of toilet paper trailing behind her. The room fell silent, a short, but awkward silence before everyone picked up their conversations and tried to act normal. Shortly afterward, the family left the table, before dessert, as if there was a cloud of shame hanging over them.

I'M DRINKING A wine from Olevano Romano, 25 miles (40 km) east of Rome, a powerful, dense red wine. I've seen it described as smelling like a mixture of plums, pomegranate, and wild boar. Such imagery can make your imagination run so wild you risk forgetting about the wine itself. The combination of adjectives can often sound more like a brothel from hell than a wine suitable for consumption in polite company. But in this case, the description of the wine is actually not entirely wrong. The wine has something a bit gamey, almost dirty, about it. The initial sips had a somewhat bitter edge, slightly reminiscent of kale, first in an unpleasant, prickly way, and then—as the wine opened up—the flavor developed slightly with each sip.

This is what good wines are like: they can smell of flowers or wet cement, but don't allow themselves to be trapped, no matter how many aromas you add. Sunburned skin, wood shavings, apple cores, and sweat. They don't necessarily taste this way or that way. Their taste can't be captured. They are constantly changing, like the clouds in the sky. The wine in my glass is made from the Cesanese grape, an ancient grape that has only managed to survive in the area around Lazio. Many believe it to be the closest you can get to the taste of a real Roman wine, and that the grape has been grown here since Roman times.

This grape is known to ripen extremely late. Harvesting it too early will give you nothing but a tasteless, juice-like wine. If the farmer waits and harvests late, on the other hand, the wine will become dense and compact, like the one I'm drinking. But it's possible that the autumn rain will come and make the entire vintage moldy. Even if it doesn't actually date back to Roman times, it's still a good example of how wine probably tasted in the old days: like a fruit squash to ordinary folks, but concentrated and perhaps quite similar to what we recognize as a good wine for those who had enough money and knowledge. In addition there were a number of fairly eccentric ideas about how wine should be made and stored back then: smoky flavors were considered particularly attractive, so some wines would be stored above fireplaces for several years. The grotesque horror of retsina—a white wine containing resin, still served in Greece today—originated from a method of preventing wine from oxidizing.

According to the Bible, Noah was the world's first winemaker. As God's wrath at his creation began to subside and the floodwaters receded, the ark made landfall on Mount Ararat, where Noah settled and immediately began farming grapes. God had chosen Noah, because he was the only virtuous man left on Earth, to continue the human race unblemished by other humans. It turned out, however, that he wasn't entirely flawless. In fact, he was what we'd characterize as quite a drunkard. A small glass with his food wasn't enough. Noah would get quite hammered and be ashamed of it afterward, but then keep drinking anyway—a pattern that's been repeated in the generations that followed.

How much truth there is in the biblical story of Noah is a matter of faith. But modern science has at least confirmed a small but important part of it: it was probably around Mount Ararat that wine was first made. To this day wild grapevines grow in the surrounding areas, what is now the border region between Turkey, Iran, and Georgia.

The Persians have a different story about the origins of wine, from roughly the same area, about King Jamsheed, who loved eating grapes so much that he once had the idea of storing them in jars so he could eat them at a later date. When he opened the jars again after a few months, the grapes had burst and juice was bubbling and frothing from them. Jamsheed suspected that some kind of dark magic, or poison, was at work and he decreed that the jars of "grape juice" must not be drunk. But a young woman in his court ignored his ban. She'd been thrown out of the king's harem and had decided to kill herself, so she began drinking some of the liquid now marked "poison." Instead of dying, she found herself becoming gradually less miserable before eventually falling asleep. When she awoke the next day, she started drinking again. Elated by what had happened, she took her discovery to the king, who forgave her and started drinking himself.

THE FIRST ALCOHOLIC drinks came about by chance. A honeycomb fell into a pool of water during a storm and lay there for a while. Later, when people found the pool and drank from it, they noticed something had happened. The water was sweet, but there was also something else about it. A bowl of grain and water that was left for a few days achieved a similar effect. Grapes, dates, and other sugary fruits fell to the ground, where they fermented by themselves. Precisely when humans started cultivating grapes or making wine, nobody knows, but it's estimated that even 8,000 years ago wine production was well underway. In Godin Tepe, an ancient Mesopotamian trading post in western Iran, archeologists found a clay pot containing remnants of tannic acid and tartaric acid—sure signs of wine production. Carbon dating shows that the pot is 7,000 years old, and it is considered the oldest of its kind. Traces of beer brewing dating back even further have been found in the same part of the world.

Wine is considered a pleasure—at best a harmless diversion, an interest that boring or snobbish people bother their friends with. At worst it is considered a corrupting force. But the alcohol itself represented something more. "The pleasures provided by wine were spiritual as well as sensory," writes Paul Lukacs in his book *Inventing Wine*. There was something ethereal about wine, or with the alcohol at least. It was a gift from above. When people drank wine, they had a magical contact with the heavens.

As my late professor the Norwegian historian Bjørn Qviller, and eventually many other historians, pointed out, alcohol—wine, beer, and in some places spirits—was absolutely central to the emergence of a number of early societies. To be a citizen of Athens, one had to own land, and large parts of the city-state's class system were built around the size of the vineyard a person controlled. The Greek drinking guild—*sympósion*—is just one of many examples of how social drinking has been important for political, intellectual, and cultural life.

It's easy to forget today, when we gather for an academic symposium without so much as a drop of alcohol present, or when we read *The Symposium* by the near-abstinent Plato, where Socrates and friends discuss love and death, that in reality the Greek symposiums were not just forums for philosophical discussions; they were proper drunken parties. Most of the time they included poetry and music, but apart from that they consisted primarily of almost endless rounds of toasts, led by a host, in which all the guests had to completely empty their cups each time. Imagine a teenage drinking game being played by the pillars of society. Descriptions of hangovers and vomiting appear regularly in classical texts, and the haze of intoxication frequently overshadows the wise thoughts and reasoning we have come to understand were the main purpose of the get-togethers. For the ancient Greeks intoxication was a portal to knowledge and insight, to something to which you wouldn't otherwise have access, and we must assume, despite the vomiting, a source of pleasure.

Herodotus—he who provided the most fanciful descriptions about the origin of spices—writes that the Persians made all their major decisions while drunk. Once the effects of the alcohol had subsided, they would reconsider the decision. If they came to the same conclusion while both sober and intoxicated, the decision was deemed valid. It was almost similar to a two-chamber parliamentary system, where all the laws must pass through both the upper house of inebriation and the lower house of sobriety.

IN A SHORT HISTORY *of Drunkenness*, Mark Forsyth refers to Göbekli Tepe, an archeological site dating back 12,000 years in what is now Turkey, where the remains of huge buildings and stone blocks weighing up to 10 tonnes have been found. There is no evidence that the surrounding area was inhabited, or that grain was grown there, but they have found the remains of containers big enough to hold over 26 gallons that contain traces of oxalate, a substance that occurs when barley and water are mixed. The hypothesis is that Göbekli Tepe was a religious meeting place where people gathered to get drunk, a city of inebriation.

The most common explanations about the introduction of farming suggest that we turned to agriculture because we wanted greater food security, but these are challenged by findings indicating that the transition from the hunter-gatherer life to an agricultural one usually had the opposite effect. Among other things, it led to increased malnutrition. Humans already had ways of ensuring they had enough to eat. What we lacked was intoxication—fun! An alternative hypothesis is that we began farming grain because we wanted to get drunk. Intoxication—from beer initially, then wine—was central to the emergence of the first religions, and it was the glue in the first relatively centralized societies. Four and a half thousand years ago, in the city of Uruk, Sumeria, they had developed eleven different beers for different occasions. Uruk socializing, according to the author Iain Gately, revolved largely around beer and beer serving. When you went to the pubs of that time, the goal wasn't just to enjoy yourself, but to get completely shit-faced. "Give me eighteen jars of wine . . . I always want to be drunk," quotes Mark Forsyth from an ancient Egyptian text. An elaborate painting inside a tomb shows a courtly lady throwing up on a maid. Intoxicating drinks were a cultural force that combined sociality and religion. "We invented farming because we wanted to get drunk on a regular basis," writes Forsyth.

Benjamin Franklin, philosopher, inventor, and one of the founders of the United States of America, argued for something similar. One of his greatest interests was wine, hence the statement: "Wine is constant proof that God loves us." But he goes further. We can see God's love for us in:

the situation it has given to the *elbow*. You see in animals who are intended to drink the waters that flow upon the earth, that if they have long legs, they have also a long neck, so they can get at their drink without kneeling down. But man, who was destined to drink wine, is framed in a manner that he may raise the glass to his mouth. If the elbow had been placed nearer the hand, the part in advance would have been too short to bring the glass up to the mouth.

Had it been closer to the shoulder, it would also have missed, he continues. One can only imagine what he'd consumed the night he wrote this.

IN THE BEGINNING, the Roman Empire was strict and ascetic. In the second century BC, 7,000 followers and suspected follow-ers of the wine god Bacchus were executed. Two hundred years later, they had nevertheless won: Rome was not only the center of the world but a heavily alcoholized city where extravagant parties were a daily occurrence and the drinking went on until late at night. Some noble Romans had their own vineyards on the outskirts of the city, such as at Olevano Romano, where my wine comes from. Wine was also imported from Greece, Tunisia, and eventually many other Roman territories. One of the most famous wine merchants of Roman times was Trimalchius, a fic-tional character in Gaius Petronius' *The Satyricon*, a work from the first century AD during the reign of Emperor Nero, which is often referred to as the world's oldest surviving novel. The story is like an eternal drinking binge where the main characters repeatedly end up in the most unfortunate situations as a result of drinking too much, and without learning a great deal. The goal was intoxication.

Of course, our relationship with wine and alcohol has changed since we first began drinking it. Think of wine clubs and magazines for aficionados, books ranking different producers and vintages. But however much other aspects of wine have evolved, intoxication is still a key element. We can pretend to drink wine because of its taste. And taste is important. The anticipation of more pleasure, a more complex flavor, and exciting aromas was why I splashed out on a wine that was more than double the price of the house's cheapest. To drink it is like upgrading to business class when flying, a more comfortable journey to the same destination. Nevertheless, the essence of a wine doesn't lie in its subtle nuances—the hints of leather and violets or wild boar and pomegranate. Wine isn't wine unless it also contains alcohol.

The couple sitting opposite me have ordered a bottle from Scarpa, the cult wine producer in Piedmont. It is one of the most expensive wines on the list, and the man's nose is permanently in his glass, searching for every little nuance of flavor—or he could be just avoiding contact with his wife, who is sitting there fiddling disgruntledly with her phone. Whether we are drinking fine or inferior wines, or whether we can distinguish between the ephemeral aromas and complex and ever-developing flavors, everyone in the room— apart from the three children at the next table—is experiencing the little buzz of alcohol that increases with every sip and every glass. *That* is what we are looking for when we drink wine. Although most of us are hoping we'll avoid crossing the often difficult-to-identify line between intoxicated and visibly intoxicated.

There are many negative sides to alcohol, and for that reason there have always been people trying to restrict it. In Europe and the United States, several attempts have been made to crack down on excessive drunkenness, culminating in the Prohibition of the 1920s, which, as we know, didn't go particularly well. Sobriety proved impossible to legislate and instead led to a crime wave and a whole range of other problems.

In the Islamic part of the world, the pressure to ban alcohol has persisted ever since the religion originated in the sixth century. The Qur'an forbids alcohol. At the same time, it promises "rivers of wine" for those who reach paradise. "This leads to the odd conclusion that a good Muslim will end up drinking more than a good Christian," writes Mark Forsyth sarcastically. "The latter has a lifetime to drink wine, the former has an eternity."

Iran—where the earliest remains of wine production have been found—was long considered one of the world's best wine countries, or at least the best outside Europe. The wine from Shiraz—which has nothing to do with the Shiraz grape—was exported and highly commended. "Drink wine. This is life eternal. This is all that youth will give you," reads a poem credited to the Iranian mathematician, astronomer, and national poet Omar Khayyam; he later describes "a season for wine, roses and drunken friends." Right up until the Islamic Revolution of 1979, visitors would talk about decadent upper-class parties, a European-style café culture in the major cities, and a relaxed and generous wine tradition in the countryside. True, the Iranians were Muslims, but they were relaxed and pragmatic. They enjoyed the benefits of life. And they did it a lot. In the mid-1970s, Iran had more area under vine than Australia, New Zealand, and South Africa combined.

Then, in 1979, the revolution drew a line under this 7,000-year-long period of Persian culture. Alcohol was banned. Vineyards were closed, and the Revolutionary Guard went round destroying equipment used for wine, beer, and spirit production. Strict penalties were also introduced for those violating the alcohol ban. In 2012, an Iranian couple were convicted of drinking for the third time. On the two previous occasions they had been sentenced to 160 lashes for the same offense. This time the punishment was for them to be "called back to Allah"—they were to be executed. The verdict was a shock and a warning to other thirsty Iranians, although it's unclear whether the couple actually were killed.

Can thousands of years of tradition be erased with a stroke of a pen? The Prohibition era in the United States wasn't terribly successful, partly because drinking was so engrained in the culture that it couldn't be legislated away. What was it like in countries that had banned alcohol more recently? A few years ago I decided to check by going to Iran in search of what, if anything, had survived of the ancient drinking culture and wine production. Rarely have I drunk so much. I found that once people had closed their front doors to the watchful eyes of the authorities, the shiny liquor bottles would soon appear. Those wealthy and sophisticated enough served imported whiskey, or cheap French supermarket wine, which—not unlike pepper in the old days—had multiplied in value during its own perilous journey into Iran. In the city of Shiraz, previously one of the centers of Persian wine production, vines grew everywhere, even outside the headquarters of the Revolutionary Guards. I met people who made unbearably bad home-brewed wine in their cellars, a beverage that required a considerable thirst for alcohol and a lot of determination to get down at all. Finally, I found a group of winemakers an hour from Shiraz who, for forty years, have continued to produce the traditional Shiraz wine, a sweet wine slightly reminiscent of southern French wines from Banyuls and Rivesaltes, intense and concentrated. To avoid being caught, the actual production itself had moved underground, literally. The wine is stored in jars or amphorae that are buried to make them more difficult for outsiders to find.

I was glad to see that this thousands-of-years-old tradition had been preserved, and I felt lucky to be sitting there behind the high fences of a rose-covered garden, tasting the wine Omar Khayyam had written about. However, I soon discovered that although the wine had been preserved, the tradition of drinking perhaps hadn't. There were none of the smelling and tasting rituals that is the norm among many serious wine drinkers I know. This wine, it turned out, wasn't there to be enjoyed but to be drunk—served in a milk glass filled almost to the brim. When I began sipping it tentatively— detecting a hint of almonds and a deep, concentrated fruitiness—I was looked at with horror. Didn't I like it? Yes, it was wonderful, I explained. Then why aren't you drinking it, man?

The correct thing to do, it turned out, was knock it back in large swigs, preferably emptying the whole glass in one big gulp. Then another, and another, like a Greek symposium without the philosophical discussion but with the occasional insult directed at the non-present mullahs, Revolutionary Guardsmen and others who made drinking difficult and dangerous. When I couldn't keep up, my host gave me a banana. It makes it easier to drink and prevents heartburn, he explained. New bottles were constantly brought out, each one older than the last. And there we sat, guzzling sweet wine and eating bananas until we were either too exhausted or had run out of things to propose a toast to. At one point we began singing, and although we didn't know any of the same songs, it didn't seem to matter.

When we were finished, and I sat there feeling slightly unwell, my host Kaveh was over the moon. "We are drunk. We are free!" he cried out.

This was quite different to any drinking binge I'd been on before, I thought while lying down to get a little rest, overwhelmed by bananas and alcohol. When I woke up, I had a much more familiar feeling: a heavy, universal, 7,000-year-old hangover.

MEAT

Many give up before reaching the main course. At La Carbonara, I've often heard Anne complain about the general decline in people's appetites. The ritualized Italian meal should consist of *antipasti*, *primi*, and then—the death blow—*secondi*. Anne estimates that no more than 30 percent of the guests make it all the way to *secondi* these days. Most stop at the pasta or jump straight to the dessert. Not me! I keep going. Since I know that a meal at La Carbonara requires a bit of effort, I've taken precautions, one being resisting the temptation of having a Roman three-hour lunch. And although I'm not exactly ravenous, after eating slightly too much bread, oily antipasto, and a pasta dish that was anything but modest, I've not quite reached the final level on the fullness scale. I'm full, but not yet *desperate*.

Secondi is the protein part of the meal. In classic restaurants this will be either fish or meat. If you're a vegetarian, you'll normally have to make do with ordering various *contorni*—side dishes. And if you don't know the Italian meal structure and how each place treats their *contorni*, it can be a short road to disappointment. This is a problem for vegetarians who for whatever reason also want to limit their carbohydrates and therefore don't eat *primi*. I've sat in good Roman restaurants where unhappy low-carb non-meat-eaters have been given a plate of fried courgettes, a plate of long-ago-wilted spinach, and a little bowl of ragingly bitter chicory—all cooked and served as naturally as possible, without herbs, without spices, to avoid outshining the protein main course, which paradoxically was what the vegetarian didn't want either. Tourists in search of authenticity appreciate this rigid approach to the meal structure, but at the same time it makes many young Italians view classic restaurants as old-fashioned and outdated. For me, Italy is an escape from the fashionable food of other big cities, while for young Italians, vegetarians, those too restless to sit down for three-hour meals, or simply curious about the food from other parts of the world, its traditional restaurants are just time warps, places where the clocks have stopped ticking.

For the main course I've ordered grilled lamb, which comes to the table on a scalding-hot plate. Where pasta dishes are an endless series of highly ritualized constructions, the *secondi*, the supposed highlight of the meal, is often no more than an encounter between heat and protein. What's usually served along the coast is fish. Out here in the country, the tradition is to eat meat.

Northern Italy is known for its beef: ragù in Emilia-Romagna, thick steaks in Florence, and hearty stews in Piedmont. Rome is located in sheep country, surrounded by hills and high land best suited to olives, grapes, and woolly animals. According to legend, the first Romans were shepherds, although much has changed since then. Nevertheless, Rome's most important cheese is still pecorino, made from sheep's milk, while lamb is the most important meat, closely followed by pork. There's plenty of beef on offer in the city, but nearly all of it comes from much further afield. When I recently ate at Federico Fellini's old regular eating place, Dal Toscano, near the Vatican, I was surprised and a little disappointed: the wine, the dishes, the waiters, and just about everything else are so proudly Tuscan that you suspect that even the wood used in the grill comes from Tuscany. But the meat, for which the place is so famous, is imported from Denmark.

Several of Rome's surrounding areas specialize in lamb, and they all claim that theirs is the best, richest, and most aromatic. One butcher at Campo de' Fiori sells meat from Viterbo, 50 miles (80 km) north of Rome, while the other sells lamb from Frosinone in the southeast. I have chosen the *costolette d'abbacchio scottadito* for my main course: three chops straight from the grill with some well-fried potatoes on the side. What might look like sloppily made food or a particularly rustic and simple dish is in fact a piece of minimalist cuisine. I'm struck by the smell of grilled meat, and something else, an extra dimension: it smells sweet, like milk.

During spring and well into the summer, the city goes spring-lamb crazy. Rome's inhabitants have retained their liking for young animals that "have not lost their virginity by eating grass," as the poet Juvenal described this exclusive phenomenon. The sensible way of raising sheep is to let the lambs graze until they are almost fully grown. This provides more meat, which in turn has a more fully developed flavor due to the animal's herb- and shrub-based diet. Young animals that have only consumed their mother's milk are—naturally—much smaller, and the meat has a completely different taste. It's not wild and complex but sweet and mild. The cutlet is also tiny compared to a regular lamb chop. On the other hand, it includes the rib, which has plenty of crispy fat and a thin slice of meat attached. No other meat offers such a mildly sweet taste and overwhelming feeling of pleasure.

Spring lamb is good, although very little of its flavor suggests that it's lamb. Could this be exactly why it became so popular? If you eat spring lamb without knowing what it is, and without seeing the revealingly small chops, you can easily mistake it for veal or another meat once considered nicer, although scarce in Rome. Only a tiny hint of the lamb flavor appears in the fat, since it's already there before the animal has started eating grass.

Today the only people with any relationship with the animals we eat are almost exclusively farm workers; although considering today's industrial meat production it's quite possible that even *they* don't. In the past, animals were a natural part of our everyday lives—even in the city.

The fountain that stood in Campo de' Fiori until the end of the nineteenth century was covered by a kind of lid. Its funny appearance gained it the name La Fontana della Terrina, or just La Terrina, because that was exactly how it looked—like a huge soup terrine. In fact the only way you could tell it was a fountain, and not just an oversized faience, was the water coming out of each end— just enough for the square's flower- and vegetable sellers to get what they needed. The soup terrine fountain was an object of ridicule and derision. Why in the world put a lid on a fountain? It seems like an instantly terrible idea, especially in a city adorned with so many beautiful and magnificent fountains. This was definitely nothing of the sort. But the lid was more than just an eccentric design that undermined the fountain's "fountaininess." It was first and foremost the response to a practical problem. The fountain was originally designed and built by Giacomo della Porta, one of the most famous architects in sixteenth-century Rome, best known for completing Michelangelo's plans for St. Peter's Basilica and the facade of the Jesuits' mother church, the Church of Gesù. In the Middle Ages, Campo de' Fiori had been reduced to a field on the city's outskirts, but by the end of the sixteenth century the neighborhood was about to make a comeback. Rich and powerful families were moving in. The prominent Farnese family built their magnificent palace, among other things, just a block away. And to signify Campo de' Fiori's new position as one of Rome's most fashionable quarters, it was given a fountain—which indeed did not have a lid. It was modern and elegant, a tremendous symbol of the area's increasing prestige, designed by della Porta himself.

This would have remained the case were it not for an inconvenient problem: it proved impossible to stop the fountain from being used for slaughtering livestock. As a consequence it was forever clogged up with wool, off-cuts, clotted blood, tendons, and whatever offal that even the Romans wouldn't eat. Flooding was also a problem, not to mention the horrible smells caused by the butchery. The solution was the soup terrine lid. It overshadowed the architect's stylistic vision and ruined any idea of it being elegant, but it at least brought the stench under control. When the fountain was moved in 1889 to make way for the statue of Giordano Bruno, it was placed outside Chiesa Nuova—the New Church—further northwest in the Pairone district, where it can still be observed in all its silly splendor.

Slaughtering animals in a fountain sounds totally insane, like a bizarre prank or something you might resort to in dire emergencies. However, a few hundred years ago nearly all meat came from animals that had been slaughtered in the immediate vicinity, which in Rome meant within the city. And why not use a fountain? In a warm country, at a time without any proper means of refrigeration—and with what nowadays would be seen as highly insufficient knowledge of hygiene—it was crucial that meat was fresh. Animals would be led from fields in the countryside to markets on the edge of the city, and from there to local butchers in the various districts, to ensure that meat and beast didn't part ways until absolutely necessary.

I've spent a lot of time in Zanzibar, and in its still distinctly unmodern capital Stone Town the meat trade operates largely on the same basis. Buying meat normally means having to walk over goats that are lying tethered and resigned to their fate. The butcher will often have an assistant whose sole task seems to be fanning the flies away from the meat that is already hanging up. Should he do a bad job, or be summoned to perform another task, the meat will immediately turn from red to black, almost totally covered with flies. There's an overwhelming smell of blood and guts and the earth is sticky. But goats aren't easily discouraged, and before long they get bored and start looking for food. For a modern consumer—used to buying meat that looks almost identical to any other neatly packaged product—it feels rather unexpected to have your trouser leg nibbled by a goat while selecting a piece of its recently deceased brother or sister to the sound of a butcher sharpening his knife in preparation for the next kill. But that's how it is when you choose to eat meat; the nibbling goat reminds me that all the meat we consume is the result of something losing its life. And that's how everyday life in Rome was, from its founding almost 3,000 years ago until the new central slaughterhouse at Testaccio was completed in the 1880s. The animal you ate for dinner had been led through the city that morning; it had let out a final desperate cry and bled to death in the street where you lived.

They say that man is the only predator that has a friendly relationship with its prey. A lion will always try to kill a gazelle should the opportunity arise; we, however, care for and protect our animals until the day—one that suits us—we take their lives because we consider it to be our right. Some are killed because they are old and no longer useful to us; others because they are young and that's when we think they taste best. We might be appalled at the thought of a meat market in Rome or Zanzibar, and be committed to better farming practices—or we perhaps don't want to think about where meat comes from at all—but we still take domestic animals for granted. They exist, almost like an extension of ourselves.

This hasn't always been the case. In fact, domestic animals have been with us a vanishingly short part of our human existence. The origins of our predecessors, the early humans today classified as *Homo*, date back 1.5 million years. *Homo sapiens*, the species of modern humans to which everyone now living belongs, has been around for roughly 300,000 years. Our unique ability to adapt has allowed us to spread to areas with totally different food sources. Even 15,000 years ago, millennia before livestock and agriculture came into the picture, we were the planet's most successful animal species. Humans existed all over our original continent, Africa, where we had adjusted to life in the equatorial jungle belt, in the highlands, along the great rivers, and in the deserts of the north and south. There were humans in Siberia and on the Indian sub-continent, in China and the Caucasus, in Papua and Australia, on many Pacific islands, in the areas of Europe not covered by ice, and from north to south in the Americas. As a broad but not all too imprecise generalization, you can say that there were humans in the same areas that are populated today, only in much, much lower numbers. Population estimates vary enormously, but most of them give something between 1 and 10 million people, all of whom were supported by the local fauna and flora. Nature dictated, while we triumphed because we were the best at adapting.

We have cohabited with animals for a mere 10,000 years, a brief moment in the long history of mankind. But the change this involved—along with the farming of grain and other plants—was absolutely crucial for humans. The domestication of animals has been as important as "the invention of stone tools, religion, written language, mathematics and the more recent industrial and information technology revolutions," writes zoologist James A. Serpell in the preface of the book *Animals as Domesticates*. Most of the progress—and many of the setbacks—of the last 10,000 years occurred with animals by our side, and none of it could have happened without them. When we grew our own food and kept livestock, we were—at least partly—disconnected from the order of nature; we turned it on its head. We were no longer *following* nature. We were *controlling* it.

Each new area we colonized was filled by our plants and our animals. We shaped nature in our own image, something which required increasingly more equipment and technology; more buildings, tools, drainage ditches, fields, roads; and eventually more towns and villages. Today, hardly any part of the world is unaffected by human hands. We have created green valleys in areas once dry, and inadvertently deserts in areas once lush, and populated the Earth with billions of hungry people and over 25 billion livestock.

How did this happen? What was it that made us take this step, from a successful life, in harmony with nature, to a completely different one based on us dominating nature?

"Ten or eleven thousand years ago, a hunting party heard a strange bleating sound," writes Brian Yarvin in his book *Lamb: A Global History*. The hunters followed the sound and found an ewe with a broken leg. Instead of killing it, they took it back to camp: "and soon they had it and a couple of baby ones as well. Those hunters were the proud owners of the first domesticated lambs. Once the lambs were born, the hunters saw a wholly different animal. Docile, almost obedient, and easy to keep." There's still a great deal we don't know about how sheep and other livestock were domesticated, but one thing is certain: it didn't happen like that. The whole process was slow and demanding, for both humans and animals.

There are many competing theories about how humans tamed what we today call domestic animals. In their book about beef, Rimas and Fraser describe what they call the "humungous pest" theory, which claims that humans—after beginning to cultivate the earth—found their newfound prosperity at risk from troublesome animals that would eat the crop before it could be harvested. Imagine finally working out how to cultivate grain, only to find that it gets eaten by marauding flocks of wild goats, sheep, and oxen. "At first, the offended farmers probably roasted and boiled the trespassers," they write. "Eventually, the farmers realized that instead of killing the trespassers, they could corral them and eat them later." Animals that were aggressive in captivity were killed first, and this led to the gradual development of calmer ones. Each new generation produced animals that were increasingly docile, until they eventually became another species: tame animals.

Another theory Rimas and Frasier discuss concerns changes in climate. A change in the weather systems caused long periods of drought in the area around the Fertile Crescent. The people living there, for whom grain farming was a relatively recent thing, had to abandon or reconsider their relationship with agriculture, but since the area was now far more populous than before, there weren't enough resources for everyone to return to a hunter-gatherer existence. Instead, shepherds would follow their flocks to the most fertile places in the vicinity. An ear of grain cannot move and will die without rain, but a herd of animals can be followed to green spots or valleys where it *has* rained, and where there's a greater abundance of human food. In addition, many livestock can graze on things that would have been inaccessible to humans otherwise, such as shrubs, grasses, and wild plants, and convert them into meat and milk. Anyone who has traveled through the arid countries of Africa and the Middle East will have been impressed by how content the goats seem with a diet of tin cans, thistles, and desert dust.

The idea that people either became farmers or shepherds, that the options were either crop farming or animal husbandry, appears several times in the region's early mythology. The most famous example of this is probably the story about the brothers Cain and Abel—Cain being a farmer and Abel a shepherd. "In the course of time Cain brought some of the fruits of the soil as an offering to the Lord," says the Old Testament's Book of Genesis. "Abel also brought an offering—fat portions from some of the firstborn of his flock. The Lord looked with favor on Abel and his offering, but on Cain and his offering he did not look with favor." Following this, Cain killed his brother in a fit of rage and jealousy. In the Middle East there are a number of groups still living as shepherds, who live wholly or partly nomadic existences, and there are still traces of conflicts between the stationary farmers determined to protect their crops and the shepherds who want their animals to graze freely. But on the whole these two groups didn't diverge. Essentially crop farming and animal farming have been compatible ways of life.

As early as the 1880s, Darwin commented on the changes that occur when wild animals are tamed. They develop characteristics that their wild relatives lack, in their appearance, psychologically and physiologically. Consider the evolution of wolf into dog; its teeth became smaller, as did its head, its coat changed color. The tame animal will often retain some childish features as an adult. Its temperament also changed significantly. From having to fight for survival, where aggression or shyness were decisive qualities, it became important for the animal to adapt to human preferences. The smartest thing an ex-wolf can do to ensure the survival of his own and new species is to fawn, wag his tail eagerly, sit devotedly at his master's feet, and respond to any discipline with a clear display of submissiveness, not resistance. Other animals use the same strategy, implemented in various ways, but most involve playing stupid, or becoming stupid, and presenting themselves as cute and non-threatening.

There is more to domesticating an animal than to taming one or two. It involves creating a beast that remains tame from generation to generation. You can tame a zebra here and a zebra there, as the eccentric nobleman and zoologist Lionel Walter Rothschild did in the late 1800s. To show off his achievements, Rothschild would drive around London in a chariot pulled by four zebras. But four tame zebras prove nothing; it is no more than a circus trick. The main reason zebras have not been domesticated is, in simple terms, because they have so many disorderly genes that a tame zebra in no way guarantees tame and sociable descendants. Even the offspring of two successfully tamed animals can be wild. Just think of all the different "lion tamer eaten by lion" articles you've read. A dog that suddenly attacks its owner is acting contrary to its nature. A lion that eats the lion tamer is more like a hypnotized person suddenly waking up and being his normal self again.

The list of animals that have been kept as pets includes jaguars, lynxes, leopards, sloths, bears, baboons, gazelles, hyenas, and antelopes. Most would agree that these animals haven't exactly dominated the world of farming. In fact, of all the different animals in existence, only a handful are considered fully domesticated: sheep, pigs, goats, cows, dogs, cats, donkeys, horses, reindeer, water buffalo, yaks, rabbits, and various types of camels, as well as their relatives llamas and alpacas. These are the animals we have fully succeeded in making our own.

Having said that, can we be sure this was something *we* did to them? In 1992, the American author and journalist Stephen Budiansky published the book *The Covenant of the Wild: Why Animals Chose Domestication*. Budiansky claims, as the title of the book indicates, that this decisive transformation wasn't the result of human involvement, but happened because these animals simply tamed themselves. Tame animals, he writes, didn't come about through the trial and error of skilled and persistent humans, but are instead the descendants of opportunistic animals that variously benefited from staying close to human settlements. Some, such as dogs, cats, and pigs, had been primarily searching for leftovers. Others wanted safety. It must have seemed like pure luck to the humans at first, an opportunity to capture their prey without going on an exhausting hunt. But we eventually found other ways of using animals, a coexistence where, instead of killing them on the spot, we created a symbiotic, albeit rather unfair, relationship. In return for meat and milk, we protected the animals from other predators, and eventually gave them food and shelter.

Some animals, such as reindeer, may also have been attracted to the nutrients in our urine. In areas that lacked natural sources of salt, Siberia for example, they would be drawn toward whatever human settlements there were at the time. "Humans had a powerful lure," writes David Sherman in his book *Animals in the Global Village*, "as the reindeer craves urine in its salt-deficient diet and is especially disposed to human urine." The same may have been the case with several other ruminant animals, such as goats, sheep, and cattle.

These theories say that it wasn't we who chose them—they chose us. It's strange to think that it perhaps wasn't our dazzling intelligence that allowed us to subjugate animals, but might have been another quality, such as our irresistible piss.

To leave one's fellow species and submit to human governance was an overriding strategy that of course had numerous drawbacks. The animals that acquiesced to humans found their own freedom drastically restricted, a deprivation of liberty that eventually affected nearly every aspect of life, from childhood and reproduction to death. That humans feel entitled to kill animals when it suits us—for example, because we like the taste of lambs that have only drunk milk—must be a recurring source of shock and disappointment to our livestock. Nevertheless, living with people had some clear benefits. We deliberately and inadvertently wiped out large numbers of the wild animals we encountered as we spread to new regions and the pressure from the growing population increased. Domestic animals, on the other hand, were not exposed to the same thing, quite the opposite: animals that competed with our domestic ones were often exterminated to make room for them. Out with the irritating antelopes, jumping too high and eating the crops. In with the docile sheep who stay behind the fence.

By living with the most dangerous of all predators, domestic animals found that they were less liable to come under random attack themselves. Over time, domestic animals became calmer and developed smaller brains, making them even more submissive and dependent on humans. Today, domestic animals exist in larger numbers than ever, and the six most common of them—pig, goat, sheep, cow, dog, and cat—are found all over the world. Not all biologists go as far as Budiansky, but many still underscore the symbiotic nature of man's relationship with animals, and how this cannot be achieved without a certain degree of cooperation from the animals. That no one has managed to tame deer or elk isn't through lack of trying, but because the animals refused or didn't see the point of entering such a long-term collaboration.

Traditionally mankind's transition from a hunter-gatherer society to cereal growers and livestock farmers has been presented as a step forward, a progression from barbarism to civilization: from our bestial origins to ruling the Earth, gods almost. After all, the cultivation of soil and taming of animals laid the foundations for the rest of human culture and its many achievements. Without agriculture and livestock, we would have remained primitive and in constant need, it was said. In recent decades, this notion has been challenged. Hunter-gatherers were just as fit and healthy as their home-dwelling offspring. They probably spent far less time hunting and gathering than the farmers spent on their often boring and monotonous work. In the generations following the introduction of agriculture, the average human height decreased and malnutrition increased. The combination of densely clustered settlements and domestic animals led to new diseases—with sometimes catastrophic effects. There were so many disadvantages that when you read authors like Jared Diamond or James C. Scott, who portray the transition to agriculture as one big mistake, you might wonder why humans took this step of settling down to till the soil at all.

Humans and animals are different, but they are similarly motivated to connect with each other. Just as most modern-day humans prefer the semi-slavery of waged labor to the unreliable liberty of freelancing, both animals and humans have throughout history chosen security over freedom. And within this self-imposed constraint lay the seed of advancement. For the lucky animals this meant the nicest stall in the barn and free access to food, which you could say equates to something like 10,000 years' worth of annual bonuses and promotions. For humans, it meant predictability and the opportunity to build up a surplus.

When humans no longer simply hunted animals but kept them as property, animals became a form of walking capital, a savings account, if you will. Even a skilled hunter-gatherer can never know when a hunt will lead to the next catch, and the security of having a walking food store must have been appealing. While grain stocks represented one type of food security and capital, animal farming represented another, equally important one. The advantage with animals was that they could take themselves to market. In good periods, the flock would grow, which meant the family, group, or clan could do so too. When times were lean, you could eat the animals, or sell them.

When I worked in Zimbabwe's capital, Harare, for six months in the year 2000, I got to know the gardener at the housing complex where I lived. He was constantly asking me for advice on how to prepare what he solemnly called his "business plan," which involved getting a loan, buying two calves, and then breeding them. Why did he specifically want to do this, I wondered. After all, he didn't own any land, and would be dependent on a pasture that belonged to his relatives. He also had a job in the city, which meant that he would have to pay someone else to look after the animals. When we factored in the costs of fodder, medicine, and animal care, our calculations never made it to zero, let alone into profit. So why this? The response to my friendly-but-critical question was equally friendly, head-shaking laughter. After all, I was a stranger. "Without cows, you are nothing," he said. Then he asked me to help him calculate everything again, hoping for a better result.

Around that same time, however, Zimbabwe was thrown into a political and social crisis that led to a prolonged and steep economic decline. During the months I was in the country there were fuel shortages and power cuts, as well as inflation, political violence, mass unemployment, and uncertainty. After I left, inflation rose and rose, peaking at 231 billion percent. Mass unemployment became something far worse: a situation where barely anyone had a job. There was also a shortage of food, in what had been one of Africa's richest countries. When I followed the developments from a distance I often thought about the gardener, and how it perhaps hadn't been such an unwise plan to buy cows as security after all.

Animals have provided meat, although for most of the time we have kept livestock their meat has been a fairly minor benefit. When they were dead these animals also provided leather that could be used for clothing and tools, and the bones, tendons, and horns were also used. In the Middle East it was common to store and transport water or wine in goatskin bags; it says wine *bags*, not bottles, in the Old Testament. But first and foremost, the animals were useful while they were alive. Cows were draft animals whose muscles had ploughed the soil and transported goods to market before being eaten. Sheep provided wool. And of course the multi-stomached animals—sheep, goats, and cows—all provided milk, which was a seemingly endless source of nourishment, and a taste we quickly became addicted to. Milk offered us another level of food security and greatly reduced the infant mortality rate. Mothers could supplement their own milk with that of the livestock, so they no longer had to breastfeed for as long, and that meant they became fertile much sooner after giving birth.

Ah, the joys of a glass of milk, of cheese, yogurt, and butter! All of them important—almost essential—parts of our lives. In fact our relationship with milk and dairy products is almost as inexplicable as our relationship with pepper. Humans don't actually tolerate milk. Initially almost everyone would lose the ability to digest milk when they became adults. But once we had access to milk from a source other than our mothers, not using it was inconceivable. We drank milk, ate cheese, and didn't give a damn how bloated we were, because the comfort we must have felt, before running out into the bush to relieve ourselves, must have been sufficient to make us want to continue. And before long these milk drinkers had drunk their way into a genetic mutation that today means we are lactose tolerant well into adulthood. Researchers from the University of Maryland, who discovered the mutation in 2006, claim this made it possible for the milk-mutants to leave far more descendants than those who were lactose intolerant, thus replacing or outcompeting them in many parts of the world. Just as there are far more domestic animals than wild ones today, there are also far more descendants of dairy eaters than of those who didn't consume milk or dairy products.

Ranking the contribution animal farming has made according to how important each animal has been is difficult. But it's easy to point out the one thing most often overlooked, the dirty secret that must have been the difference between poverty and abundance: excrement. Not only were animals another branch of farming, but in most places animal farming was also a necessity for there to be any cultivation at all. In a few places, such as Mesopotamia, along the Nile, and sections of the great rivers of Asia, the annual floods provided a regular top-up of new, nutrient-rich soil. But these self-fertilizing super-regions were the exception, and that's where excrement came in. Without manure, farming was only half as powerful, in fact not even that much. On the island of Papua in Oceania, agriculture developed entirely independently of what happened in the Fertile Crescent and in China. Unfortunately, the large animals that once existed in Papua had long since gone extinct, so its farmers had to make do without draft animals and, more crucially, without manure. When Europeans and other colonialists reached the island's interior in the mid-twentieth century, they found what they described as a Stone Age society, built primarily around sweet-potato farming. A couple of years ago I visited Papua's swampy lowlands myself, where its inhabitants practiced a kind of migrating slash-and-burn method—clearing farmland with fire—as well as the hunting and harvesting of protein-rich larvae. The lack of fertilizer makes it impossible to live in the same place for more than a few years; when the land is drained of nutrients, the inhabitants have to move on. It's a good life in many ways, but a hard one, and not least a life where building up any kind of food reserve will be difficult, because, to some degree, you have to deal with the combined disadvantages of being both hunter-gatherer and farmer.

In India, where large sections of the population are vegetarian, one of the reasons for cows still being appreciated—and perhaps the very reason they were considered sacred in the first place—was because they were needed to fertilize the soil. On a trip to India, I visited a farmer who runs an organic farm in Rajasthan, a few hours from the capital, Delhi. Like most Indians, she too was a vegetarian, but she still had cows, which provided some milk that was used to make yogurt and *ghee*—clarified butter. But the most important thing the animals contributed, she explained, was urine and excrement. Used in combination with crop rotation, it guaranteed fertile soil year after year. Some of the cow muck was also dried and burned to repel insects and pests. This way of operating was the rule until the introduction of synthetic fertilizers and pesticides stripped the Indian cows of their purpose. They are still considered sacred, but since they are no longer as useful, and hence are not afforded so much care and attention, many of them now wander the streets, as stray and skinny deities.

After taming animals, our diet went through a rather paradoxical change: we began eating far less meat. From being a major food source for most hunter-gatherers, meat became a rarity, more like an afterthought. The meat from wild animals had cost us nothing; as long as we managed to kill them, it was pure gain. Domestic animals, however, were guarded and fed—and most of them also performed a range of tasks for us. Meat was something eaten on special occasions, when there was a party or during a religious holiday. Even the diets of wealthy Romans were overwhelmingly vegetarian. The French historian Florence Dupont points out that most Mediterranean cultures had a sacrificial tradition around meat; something we still see in Islam and Judaism, where the animals had to be killed ritualistically for the meat to be considered a sanctioned food. This was also the case in Rome. When meat was put on the table, it was the result of a sacrifice made to the gods. The poor, on the other hand, couldn't afford to eat meat. They could hope to get a taste of it now and then during the large public parties where it was distributed, but as you can imagine, the best cuts never ended up on the poor tables. The Roman poet and satirist Juvenal wrote about a Roman slave who thought longingly about the sow's womb he once tasted at an inn. Spring lamb would have been beyond his wildest dreams.

"For two million years we were hunters; for ten thousand years we were farmers; for the last one hundred years we have been trying to deny it all," writes Stephen Budiansky. We have eaten meat for as long as we have been human, perhaps even longer, but we have never had less knowledge of where this meat comes from. How many in the prosperous and "developed" world have plucked a chicken, or experienced what it's like to rip the guts out of a freshly slaughtered bird? In terms of human history, this was until a moment ago a requirement for getting meat onto the table. Today, very few people have had a whole chicken in the kitchen. We know what animal beef comes from, but we still don't see beef as part of a cow, it's just beef. And it's perhaps no wonder, because in Europe and North America, no more than 2 percent of the population currently live on farms with livestock.

What's paradoxical about this lack of closeness to animals is that meat consumption has simultaneously exploded. My grilled spring lamb chops could have been on a menu for the Roman upper class 2,000 years ago. But although I don't normally eat spring lamb, it's absolutely normal for me to eat meat. It is no longer reserved for special occasions. Many people eat meat every single day—even several times a day. Meat is everywhere, for breakfast, as a sandwich filling, in abundance at the canteen, for lunch and dinner, fast food, comfort food, or snack and party food. In the United States, an average of over 265 pounds (120 kg) is eaten per person per year. In Italy the figure is almost 200 pounds (90 kg), while in the United Kingdom it's around 187 pounds (85 kg). Most of this meat comes from animals that have never had human contact, that have never set foot in the wild, and have perhaps never seen daylight. Normally we won't have seen the animals either, until they are neatly cut, pale-pink products in the store.

When I took over the no longer active family farm in southern Norway fifteen years ago, I tried reviving the animal husbandry that had ceased there at some point in the 1950s. My goal wasn't to become a farmer but to gain a slightly broader understanding of food production and where food comes from. In the summer I kept a mix of chickens, ducks, sheep, goats, and pigs. And even though it was always a hobby project, I became familiar with several of the challenges that come with keeping livestock, plucking the ducks' long wings so they wouldn't fly away, constantly repairing the fence, and capturing runaway sheep while apologizing to my neighbor, who was more fond of his rose bushes than he was of woolly animals. During the first year, I had a goat that didn't have enough milk for its two kids, Saftis and Tyggis, which meant they grew up being bottle-fed by a substitute mom—me. What I got in return for this service was complete devotion. The two little goats followed me everywhere, and would jump up on my lap when I sat at the table outside. But as Tyggis entered puberty the young billy goat began showing increasingly unruly behavior. He gored our ducks and chickens, harassed his sister, chased the chickens, and tried to mate with his mother. The solution to the growing problem was to take him behind the barn and shoot him. One moment he was following me on an adventure, the next he was bleeding and convulsing on the ground. Then, as I skinned the carcass, he was gradually transformed, from the goat I knew and cared for, into cuts of meat. I don't think I was fully prepared for my dramatic evolution from provider to executioner, and in the evening, when he appeared on the table garnished by herbs and potatoes, it took a while to get used to the change we had both gone through.

ROMANS ARE PROUDLY well mannered, often bordering on snobbish, and fiercely critical of uncouth people with inferior customs. You'll see them eating pizza with a knife and fork, something which is both absurd and impractical but considered the only cultured thing to do. When I give up the cutlery in favor of my hands and start gnawing on the lamb chop, I know it's not terribly good manners. But it's the only way to get at most of the meat while it's still crispy and deliciously fatty. I savor the taste while feeling a tiny pang of a guilt. Of course, in order for us to eat meat an animal must be killed . . . But a lamb that hasn't yet explored the world, taken straight from its mother's breast? It's brutal, although not quite as brutal as eating a young goat who thinks you're its mother.

The combination of pleasure and shame reminds me of the little ortolan, a bird much favored by French gourmands, which is caught, then kept in the dark while being fattened up. It is then literally drowned in armagnac and baked in the oven.

To eat it one must follow a ritual. A large napkin is placed over the head of the person about to eat the bird, who then eats it in one go, entrails and all—while continually keeping their head covered. The napkin is there partly to capture the full aroma of the bird, but also to "hide this shameful and decadent act from the eyes of God." Chomping away on my baby lamb, I realize that I should perhaps ask for a large napkin myself to savor the aromas and hide my manners from my fellow guests. I scan the room, but I'm not getting any dirty looks. There's no lightning bolt from above either; our Lord must have become used to the human tradition of killing innocent animals for pleasure. Throughout the evening I also notice several other guests putting their knives and forks down to gnaw on the tiny pieces of lamb, with the kind of hunger that comes when you are full but nevertheless roused by something so good you forget all about the meal's previous excesses.

FIRE

Rome has seven pilgrimage churches. San Lorenzo fuori le Mura is the only one I can enter as a true pilgrim, not just a tourist, and, in some ways, a believer. The church is located, as the name more than suggests, outside the old city walls—*fuori le Mura*. It's hardly the most beautiful in the city. From the outside, it looks more like a cross between a saloon and a Roman temple. During the Second World War, in July 1943, it was among the relatively few ancient buildings subjected to Allied bombing; this destroyed the facade and parts of the entrance. It was rebuilt in the decades that followed, and although the new facade is an exact replica of the original, the result still looks a tiny bit like a movie set, a combination of a western and a gladiator film, as if the leftovers of both films had been stored on top of each other at the end of filming. The interior is a chaotic mix of the grandiose and the austere, the best—or second best—from several different eras. There are triumphal arches, cherubs, frescoes, and Byzantine mosaics, along with gold leaf and alabaster. A number of tombs, sarcophagi, and altar niches provide final resting places to dignitaries such as rich benefactors, popes, and prime ministers.

But there is no doubt who the most important person in the building is. The church is built on what's said to be the spot where the Roman deacon Lawrence—Lorenzo in Italian—was executed in the year AD 258. Consequently—in addition to the obvious religious significance—it's also possible to view the place as a cathedral dedicated to the most fundamental element of a meal: fire—the primordial power of cooking. Without fire, bread would not have been bread, the artichoke just a bitter-tasting thistle, and carbonara would have been a collection of partly inedible components. And the lamb chops—which I'm now enjoying—would have none of the flavor and tenderness: they would be tough and pallid.

DURING THE REIGN of Emperor Valerian, from 253 until 260, the Roman Empire experienced some of its first bouts of decline through loss of territory, recurring plague, and social unrest. Valerian himself was captured by the Persians, forced to die by drinking molten gold, then flayed and stuffed. However, before that, he had instructed that all Christians who wouldn't submit to the Roman gods should be executed. As archdeacon of the underground Christian congregation Lawrence was responsible for its treasury. When he was told to hand over all the Church's money to the state, he responded by distributing it to the poor instead. This irritated the authorities so much—although *irritated* perhaps isn't exactly the right word—that they decided not only that Lawrence should die, but that he should die in a spectacularly painful way. Crucifixion, beheading, and stoning were the most popular execution methods at the time. However—given that Lawrence's crime was both economic and religious—none of them were considered punitive enough. Instead, an enormous gridiron was constructed, to which Lawrence was fastened before it was placed over red-hot coals. According to legend, Lawrence didn't seem to notice the heat at all, but just lay there on the gridiron without giving any indication that he was in pain. His last words to the executioners are said to have been: "I'm quite well done now. Turn me over and take a bite." Lawrence was later canonized, and is today considered the patron saint of grill chefs—and comedians.

In several Catholic countries, it's common to name grill restaurants after St. Lawrence—or San Lorenzo. I did the same thing when I opened a small grill restaurant in Oslo with some friends ten years ago. At St. Lars—as Lawrence is called in Norwegian—there is a huge painting by Tor-Arne Moen depicting St. Lars on the gridiron over the fire. The food served is almost exclusively grilled.

Although I understand that there's perhaps a degree of exaggeration in the story of Lawrence, walking around this large church still fills me with awe. Wherever you look there are small statues of the saint—a pale, rather anonymous-looking man, although instantly recognizable from the gridiron he instructively carries in his hand. At the opposite end of the entrance, beside the steps leading down to the crypt where Lawrence's remains now lie, I see the shrine with the very gridiron that was supposedly used for his execution. On August 10 each year, the feast day of St. Lawrence, his charred skull is brought out and displayed. Hanging from the wall of the church is the stone he was laid on, which still bears the marks of his burnt body. It is macabre and at times beyond absurd. Are you supposed to be shocked or amused? Is it tragic or funny?

There is a deeper aspect to this story. Apart from all the embellishments, the man with the gridiron is an important reminder of our shared human origins. Not on the grill, thankfully. But right beside it, as chefs.

TODAY GRILLING HAS evolved into a popular hobby for men who wouldn't otherwise dare, or want to, set foot in a kitchen. There are grills the size of Cadillacs, and countless forums on the Internet where procedures and techniques are discussed in detail. Gas grills compete with American smokers, and specialty charcoal made from hickory and other hardwoods is mailed by overnight express around the world to home chefs eager to impress. No other form of cooking has increased so much in popularity in recent years, and hardly anyone is so obsessed with equipment. Grilling is fashion, a sign that you keep up with the times.

This makes it easy to forget what grilling actually is: the first and most important cooking technique. Since the dawn of time, fire has been a part of, yes, a requirement for, our meals. The taste and smell of grilled food—the unique combination of smoke and fat—is food's primeval flavor. And it's quite probable that we are genetically programmed to recognize and like both.

The intense heat from red-hot embers triggers several browning and caramelization processes in food, such as the Maillard reaction, a chemical reaction between carbohydrates and amino acids. Although few people care to study what happens when meat is heated on a molecular level, there is hardly anyone who doesn't somehow understand what's going on. Think of a steak, or some delicious little chops. Raw or cooked? Boiled or grilled? You know the taste just by thinking about it.

PERSONALLY, I LIKE meat to be grilled on a scorching heat. When grilling steak or any other beef cut, I try to wait until the meat has a nice, crispy texture before turning—not completely burned, but I don't want it *not* burned either. When grilling lamb shank at St. Lars, we cook the meat for a long time at a low temperature, to denature the proteins and tenderize it without losing its juiciness, and then we grill it on an extremely high heat. To emphasize the point, and to include some of the fire from the grill in a nod to the very first meal, we stick a burning sprig of rosemary into the meat just before serving. The idea is for the blazing sprig to fill the dining room with smoke and remind the guests, including those at the neighboring tables, of a fire somewhere way, way back in time. Plus, we just love playing with fire.

The hunt for food is a leitmotif for most living creatures. There is something extraordinary about how a group of lions will gather around a buffalo or giraffe they have killed, or how butcherbirds will impale poisonous insects on thorns and wait for the venom to be neutralized before eating them. But no animal actually *cooks*; only humans do that. And no animal has meals, as we recognize them in all human cultures and societies.

WHAT WAS THE first meal? When did it take place? To find the answer we have to return to the first humans. The step from apes to humans was made slowly, gradually, and in fits and starts—first to early humans, *Homo*, who had a different physiology and mental capacity than our more primitive relatives and predecessors, and then to modern humans, *Homo sapiens*. The last of our relatives, the Neanderthals and the Denisovans, died out roughly 40,000 years ago. Common to all humans, both those alive today and those who lived before us, is a unique brain that allows us to form complex social structures.

Two years ago, in a rare case of my wife's and my own field-work coinciding, we visited a cave together outside Kimberley in South Africa's barren and arid northwest, toward the border of the Kalahari Desert. Wonderwerk Cave, as it's called, is where some of the oldest-known remains of controlled fire have been discovered.

The church San Lorenzo fuori le Mura may be dedicated to the patron saint of grill chefs, but this 480-foot-deep (145 m) cave is where it all began. It was here—and a number of other, similar places in southern Africa—that we gathered around a fire for the first time and prepared our first grilled meal. It is the cathedral of all mankind. It was here we became human.

The roof of the cave was pitch black. In places there were gray-white areas, speckled with pink where salts had penetrated and started to crystalize. There were cave paintings on the walls that were hundreds, maybe thousands, of years old: one depicting an elephant, another that could have been some kind of antelope. The cave has, with several interruptions, been inhabited for almost 2 million years. And all its inhabitants, both animal and human, have left their mark, so there is layer upon layer consisting of the remnants of their existence. In the middle of the cave archeologists had excavated an area where the rows of layers had been revealed like the growth rings of a tree. About halfway up the side of the excavated hole was a blue mark indicating a layer that dated back 1 million years. A bit lower there was a white layer that turned out to be ash from a campfire that dated back 1.5 million years.

THE CLASSIC PORTRAYAL of human history describes our evolution from apes to humans as a process that was largely due to an inherent cunningness that enabled us to constantly master new things. As Reay Tannahill writes in her book *Food in History* from 1973:

As time passed the ground-dwelling apes made specific adjustments to suit their new environment. They learned to kill or stun what they hunted by throwing stones at it, a technique that encouraged them to move on three, and then two, legs instead of four. Their wits became sharper and their brains larger as they competed with the lion, hyena and saber-toothed cat that shared their hunting grounds. Their teeth, no longer a primary weapon, changed shape, which ultimately led to the development of human speech. And their forefeet adapted into hands capable of making and using tools.

It's not a unique portrayal. You'll find it in most books describing the birth of mankind—those excluding divine intervention at least—but it is, in all likelihood, fundamentally wrong.

This portrayal assumes that we were smart from the very beginning—smart enough to begin doing smart things, like controlling fire and using tools. But how did we become so mentally sentient? The explanation says nothing about that. Nor does it adequately describe the physical transformation from early humans to modern humans. You would hardly think you'd get smaller teeth from competing with saber-toothed tigers.

THE FINDINGS AT Wonderwerk Cave help lend credence to an explanatory hypothesis that has gained more attention in recent years; one that sets the story of human creation in the kitchen. Or, more specifically, around the campfire.

Generation follows generation, and throughout the enormous time span that Wonderwerk Cave was inhabited, its inhabitants underwent the dramatic transformation into modern humans: they developed smaller jaws, a different digestive system—and, most importantly, larger brains.

The explanatory model ape→bigger brains→fire was more or less widely accepted until recently. Although, as mentioned, it had a few weaknesses. As more remains of early types of human were found, it became clear that this development had not been as steady and gradual as had previously been assumed.

There was no great difference in the brain sizes of the first bipedal monkeys, which lived 5 to 6 million years ago, and *Homo habilis*, the first representative of *Homo*, which lived about 2 million years ago. Then, about 1.5 million years ago, a new type of human appeared with a brain nearly twice as big. *Homo erectus* had smaller teeth, and a body quite similar to ours, and is considered a direct ancestor of modern man. Something had happened. What had been *human-ish* was about to become *human*. In 1999, the primatologist Richard Wrangham presented his controversial explanation for the creation of modern man, which he called *the cooking hypothesis*. Wrangham believed that it was not modern humans who, as a result of being so highly evolved, started to control fire. It was instead an early hominin—a monkey, roughly speaking—that first taught itself the art. Fire enabled us to make previously inedible food edible, which in turn gave us access to a greater supply of nutrients. And our brains grew. We were transformed. Wrangham's hypothesis broke with established knowledge and, as expected, was met with a lot of opposition. At first, the skeptics had a simple job: in 1999, there had been no discoveries of controlled fire stretching far enough back in time to establish the sequence ape→fire→bigger brains. There were discoveries in Gesher Bene Ya'akov in Israel during the early 2000s showing traces of controlled fire dating back as far as 750,000 years, and this strengthened his hypothesis, but it was still far from widely accepted.

The wonders of Wonderwerk were discovered by the archeologist Peter Beaumont. He was eighty years old when we met him, a frail and skinny widower, living with his dog in a bungalow on the outskirts of Kimberley. Beaumont started digging at Wonderwerk in 1979, and has since then been responsible for most of the cave's major excavations. It didn't take him long to realize that the discoveries were so old that they had the potential to change our understanding of human history. He believed that the remains of early fire use must be much older than previously thought. However, it took more than two decades—from the time Beaumont first claimed to have found signs of fire that were a million years old—before this was finally confirmed using modern methods of analysis. New discoveries and methods show that the earliest discoveries of controlled fire in the cave date back 1.5 million years.

AS HUMAN BEINGS, our superhero quality is that we are not mere functions of our physical needs. We are curious. We challenge our instincts and have a desire to unfold, to create. We're not satisfied with having enough to eat. We want our food to taste good. If we have fulfilled our basic needs and find ourselves with half an hour to spare, we'll start drawing, dancing, singing, telling each other stories, and playing with fire. There have also been several other very early indicators of "modern human behavior" at Wonderwerk. Halfway into the cave you will find what are probably the oldest known beds; grasses and other soft plants that were used as sleeping mats for humans who'd become a bit picky and no longer wanted to live like animals. Remains of ochre, probably used as a color pigment for body paint and decoration, have also been found. Pebbles, engraved stones, and crystals were brought into the cave with no visible function except for being decorative—they pleased us by being beautiful to hold and behold. What's more human than makeup, affectations, and art?

Fire gave us more than food. Around the fire we had heat and light, and there, lit by the flames—with our increasingly large brains, smaller teeth, and a physique that made it easier to create more advanced sounds—we began talking to each other. Food became more than just nutrition. It became a social gathering point.

In Greek mythology, Prometheus is the god of fire, and also a god with strong human sympathies. Prometheus gave humans fire, and by doing so enabled their culture to develop. Plato refers to Prometheus as the creator of humanity, because without fire we would still be two-legged apes living in caves, at best—although we wouldn't have reflected much on this, since we wouldn't have been able to. According to Richard Wrangham, the most important transformation did not take place out on the hunt but around the fire. Wrangham's hypothesis reached a large audience through his popular book *Catching Fire*, which came out in 2009. Like popular-science writers such as Jared Diamond, Wrangham bolstered his hypothesis by selecting research from a variety of fields. Among other things, he points out that modern raw-food diets—which are in some ways similar to how people ate before fire made an entrance—lead to more or less constant malnutrition for today's humans, who have a different digestive system and larger brain. Although modern-day raw-food adherents have access to virtually limitless amounts of food from different parts of the world, far more than humans long ago, even this improved diet, according to Wrangham, regularly causes women to miss their periods and a number of other symptoms indicating that your body is running on empty. While it might be a fairly sensible weight-loss strategy for those living in a modern, affluent society, it would not have been a diet conducive to the development of a larger and more energy-consuming brain. The food that was cooked over the fire was the key. Fire and cooking gave us the nourishment required for us to take the final step in this development. They transformed "the Cooking Ape" into mankind as we know it.

In other words, according to Wrangham, we are all descendants of the world's first cooks. Fire, which made food safe to eat and laid the foundation for nearly all the development and technology that followed, from the smelting of metal to the combustion engine and weapons, has been described as "mankind's greatest discovery." It gave modern humans the fuel to make many of our ideas and desires a reality, to expand our dominance over the Earth, and gave us things our ancestors could never have imagined. We created a wonderful world in our own image. And a growing layer of coal dust, which archeologists like Beaumont are analyzing, reveals how we did it.

At the same time, the rising concentrations of carbon dioxide in the atmosphere indicate just what it might cost us.

Climate change has made South Africa's dry and hot north-western region even drier and hotter. It is increasingly claimed that the area is no longer suitable for farming, perhaps not even for human habitation. When I visited Beaumont at his house on the outskirts of Kimberley, the thermometer showed 111°F (44°C). The authorities had declared a state of emergency due to the heat and drought that had been worsening year after year. More than 50,000 livestock had been sent for emergency culling due to the lack of grazing areas, and the news reported that people were dying from heatstroke.

Toward the end of our conversation, I asked the old archeologist if he'd ever thought about how they must have lived, the humans in the cave he had spent his whole life digging in. "To be honest, there hasn't been much time for that," he replied. "When the working day was over, after ten hours or more of excavating, the day still wasn't over. I then had to cook. And I'm a terrible cook. No matter what I make I always end up burning the food." He began to laugh. First quietly, then he chuckled, then we all did. After 1.5 million years of human progress, he had come no further than burning his food. There was a loud bang from the corrugated iron roof, which was constantly expanding in the heat, and Beaumont became serious once more. "Fire set mankind on the path we're on now. Fire gave us everything. And what have we done with it? We've driven the whole planet to hell! We've burned it up! That's how I see it in my old age."

I GNAW ON the last of my lamb chops, savoring the charred meat closest to the bone. This was surely what it tasted like the first time a young animal was killed and cooked over the fire, when someone gnawed on the meat and fat, delighted at how surprisingly tender it was. And around that fire there would have been many of the same elements that we enjoy today; prepared food, social inter-action, gossip and comfort, shelter, and light. Although—as Peter Beaumont said when I visited him just before he died—we were also sowing the seeds of our own destruction.

LEMON

Now. I. Am. *Desperate.* I have tried eating slowly, and I have chosen—by Roman standards—a fairly moderate menu. And yet I am so full that I can't possibly take another bite. My stomach is simply bursting with food, and at one point it feels like my whole body is full, all the way to my feet, my knees and my fingertips. I should never have gnawed on that chop. I regret it. But I still can't stop myself rubbing the last potato around the plate so I can savor the remaining drops of fat and juice.

It's been only two hours since I arrived at La Carbonara feeling ravenous, and now I can't even remember what it feels like to want food, let alone the dizzy hunger that can make you feel totally discharged or give you a moment of clarity. The thought of flipping through a menu or cookbook unable to choose, because it all looks like exactly what I want, couldn't have been further from my mind. At the same time, I know that my hunger hasn't left me for good. It always comes back, like a faithful dog. Tomorrow morning it will return, perhaps more devoted than ever because of the excess I've indulged in today. And that's what it's like, every day of our lives. Hunger is with us from the moment we are newborns looking for a breast until we reach the end of our lives. When our hunger no longer returns, there's not much else you can do except wait for the inevitable.

It's still full on the ground floor of La Carbonara. The last guests arrived just before 9.30 p.m. when the kitchen stopped taking orders and are now just finishing their *antipasti*. Dario has already donned his motorcycle helmet and exited the same way he arrived—not as the restaurant's friendly proprietor, but as a dark shadow through the dining room. A slow procession of satisfied guests comes down from the second floor. Out in the square the competing bars play music as loud as they can, until they have to turn the volume down at some point around midnight.

I'm asked if I would like dessert, and reply "No," perhaps a little more brusquely than I'd intended.

"No, not a chance!" I do not have much of a sweet tooth and normally just order a bit of cheese. Or another glass of wine. Come to think of it, my bottle is almost empty. How did that happen? Even though I waved the dessert menu away, Anne returns to ask if I'm sure I don't want some ice cream and sorbet.

"We have a very special dish, brand new, a composition of basil ice cream, lemon sorbet and . . ."

"Lemon sorbet?"

My weak point in the world of desserts.

"Yes, with lemons from Amalfi."

So much for my principled stand.

"I'll take it. But just the lemon sorbet. One scoop. Not the other things."

NOBODY KNOWS WHAT the very first lemon tasted like, but what's at least fairly certain is that it wasn't coveted for its sourness. Its juice was no doubt sour, but no one cared about that. The juice wasn't the reason it was grown in the first place. For the first few thousand years it was the most sought-after fruit because of the essential oil in its peel, which you'll notice if you rub a lemon or finely grate the peel; it is sweet, fragrant, intense, and fleeting. Lemon was used in perfume and to a degree in medicine, but it probably wasn't considered edible. Citrus fruits probably originated from the area around Assam, in far east India near the border with China. Others say they originated further west, in what is today Kashmir. Either way, it was the Chinese who first began cultivating lemons on a large scale. The most popular at the time was the thick-skinned variety, *Citrus medica* or cedrat. The fruit had a wrinkled peel and its zest was the reason why it was cultivated. The rest, the thick white layer of sponge-like pith and the tiny fruit core at the center with its seeds and bitter taste, was considered unnecessary extra material—in much the same way that we regard lemon peel today. Since the zest was the fruit's gold, Chinese farmers found ways of genetically modifying it. By constantly selecting specimens with extra thick, wrinkled skins, they were able to get more oil from each lemon. The most extreme variant is called the Buddha's hand, which has a segmented skin that protrudes from the fruit like fingers.

At first, it was normal to assume that lemons didn't arrive in Europe until the Arabs brought them some time in the ninth or tenth century. But when murals depicting citrus trees were found in Pompeii, it became clear that it must have happened much earlier, probably at the same time as the spices and other exotic goods that were being imported, perhaps as early as the first century BC. Wealthy Romans also liked having pots of lemon trees at the entrances to their houses. These evergreen trees were a decorative element throughout the year, and the small, white and intensely fragrant blossom offered protection from the smell of the street. But their fruits were just decorative elements, much like they are on the little citrus trees people have in their lounges today.

The lemon as we know it, the one that's primarily eaten or made into juice, came to Europe with Arab traders almost a thousand years later. By then, Chinese and Arab peasants had similarly modified the fruit, just as they did with the Buddha's hand—although with the opposite intention. This time they had cultivated a fruit that would have as much juice as possible, juice that was sour but aromatic, and more sweet than bitter.

LEMON TREES WERE sought after but extremely difficult to grow. The early varieties required a very special climate and fertile soil to produce a harvest of commercial quality. Cold, heat, drought, too much water or wind, too much soil, or too rich soil: any of these things could ruin the taste of the juice or cause imperfections in the skin, and would therefore affect the fruit's shelf life. As a consequence it was considered nearly impossible to make the trees into anything other than pretty, ornamental plants.

Around this time large parts of the southern Mediterranean were controlled by the Arabs, who found that lemon trees thrived particularly well in a few limited parts of their realm, mainly around Palermo and a few other places in Sicily. Successful citrus groves were established in those areas, and soon the fruit was being exported from Sicily to the Italian mainland. Even after the Arabs had been defeated in the northern Mediterranean and forced to leave Sicily the lemon business flourished. Throughout the eighteenth and nineteenth centuries, lemon became an international export commodity. It was also found that sailors who ate lemon or lime didn't get scurvy, a disease caused by the lack of vitamin C, and so from 1795 citrus fruits became a regular part of the British sailor's diet. Other countries followed suit, which created an almost explosive demand that sent the lemon even further around the world. After a stint as a medicine, it then arrived in the home. First in the kitchens of the wealthy, then those of the more general sections of the population, in Europe and the United States, where it was welcomed as a much-needed flavoring in a cuisine that must have often seemed dull and monotonous by today's standards—perhaps even by those of the time. Once lemon began appearing, like a breath of fresh air, in dressings, cakes, and sauces, there was no going back. It went from being something you never knew existed to something you couldn't—or wouldn't—do without. Furthermore, lemon—in contrast to what pepper did for rotten meat—*could* save partly spoilt fish. The explanation of how is something I snapped up in my molecular gastronomy days: if the fish isn't totally fresh or has been stored in too warm a place, it tends to develop an ammonia-like odor, the musty part of that fishy smell. This is due to a substance called trimethylamine oxide, which is a sign that the fish is beyond the limit of what's pleasant to eat. But that doesn't mean that all is lost. Trimethylamine oxide reacts with the acid found in lemon juice, and forms a similar but odorless substance, so as long as the contamination just manages to reach the surface, the fish is otherwise fine. Imagine how welcome this must have been at a time before the creation of the refrigerator, when the fish had been transported from the coast on horseback.

By the middle of the 1800s, lemon exports had become Sicily's most important source of income. And what else was it that emerged in Sicily in the 1800s? Yep, the Mafia. This was no random coincidence. In his book about the Sicilian Mafia, *Cosa Nostra*, the British author and historian John Dickie writes about the Sicilian Dr. Galati, who in 1872 inherited a 10-acre (4 ha) citrus grove on the outskirts of Palermo. Lemon cultivation was then sixty times more profitable than any other farming activity, even more so than wine production in the most prestigious wine regions of France. Galati's citrus grove was state-of-the-art: the trees were watered using a steam-powered pump operated by a full-time engineer. The facility also had a caretaker and no doubt several workers who aren't mentioned in the story. However, Galati one day suspected that some of his crop, as well as the coal that was meant to fuel the pump, had been stolen. There was good reason to think that the caretaker was behind the theft, and when he was eventually fired, unsavory things started happening. Galati received several threatening letters, and two of the men hired to be the new caretakers were killed. More letters arrived, explaining that the original caretaker was an "honorable man" and wanted to be reinstated in the job he had lost so unjustly, an obvious case of blackmail, backed by a clearly demonstrated willingness to commit violence. The doctor did not relent, however, and instead sent a series of written complaints to the police chief, who was either complicit in the whole thing or simply looked the other way. When nothing happened, Galati took his problem to the minister of the interior in Rome. All this nagging led to a number of investigations, and despite none of them leading to anything being done, it became clear during the process that the lemons weren't just being pilfered by individual crooks. Galati had uncovered a huge criminal network.

IN THE DECADES following Italy's unification in the 1860s until the beginning of the twentieth century, the Mafia, as the network became known, succeeded in expanding from a gang of local criminals to a powerful organization that had a hand in most things. For a long time the Mafia was believed to have arisen from the high level of poverty in the Sicilian countryside; the idea was that the lack of opportunities forced young, unemployed men into a life outside the law. A few years ago, Alessia Isopi at the University of Manchester and Professor Ola Olsson at the University of Gothenburg began researching Sicily's economic development at the end of the 1800s. One thing they did was compare the spread of the Mafia in different parts of Sicily with maps of areas that practiced different types of agricultural production. It soon turned out that common to all the places where the Mafia arose early on was the production and trade of lemons. Just as criminal gangs are emerging around the oil fields and diamond mines of African countries with poor state control, the Mafia emerged in the richest areas, those producing lemons, not the poor ones.

THE MAFIA DEVELOPED an intricate system in which they controlled most parts of the lemon business. It started with some of what Galati experienced: thefts and demands for protection money to ensure there would be no "accidents" in the lemon groves. In the period after Italy's unification, Sicily was on the verge of becoming a lawless place. The island had been ruled by a few centrally positioned noble families, but when they lost their power and influence the feudal system collapsed without another well-functioning authority replacing it. Crime reigned, and the Mafia was both the driving force of the problem and a kind of solution to it. Most people turned out to be more pragmatic than the principled Galati. For them, it was better to pay the Mafia a share of the profits than to risk their entire crop being stolen, either by independent thugs, or in revenge by the Mafia. It was, to quote *The Godfather*, an offer they couldn't refuse. For the farmers, it was hardly any different from what they were used to. They had previously paid money to a noble Don; now they were paying to a new Don who was maybe a little rougher at the edges but at the same time perhaps better at showing them the benefits they got in return. "Of course I can help find a job for your nephew!"

But greed begets greed, and crime begets crime; it didn't take long before the original, local gangs expanded into other businesses. There was extortion, violence, and corruption, but there were also what would appear to be normal business operations. The Mafia was everywhere. John Dickie quotes the reform politician Leopoldo Franchetti, who upon visiting Palermo in 1876 wrote: "After a certain number of these stories, the scent of orange and lemon blossom starts to smell of corpses." But the exposure of the Mafia did not stop it. As brutal as it was, the profits were formidable. The organization grew, and Sicily was no longer enough. The Mafia took control of lemon shipments and the ports before eventually accompanying their goods across the Atlantic. There they established new Mafia families who maintained their connection with the original families and their business. When the American Mafia widened its activities to include drugs, the first shipments of narcotics were smuggled in lemon cans. As economist Tim Worstall wrote in *Forbes*: "Everyone got the lemons to cure scurvy but we got another plague in return."

WHEN WE HUMANS have what we need to survive we soon become preoccupied with how to acquire things we don't need, things that offer just a little more pleasure—luxury, quite simply. One of the most luxurious things you could eat previously had nothing to do with taste, at least not in the narrowest sense: it was about eating something cold when it was hot outside. An ice cream or a glass of white wine after a day at the beach will still evoke this sense of luxury. Imagine how it must have been to be served something cold in a boiling hot and filthy city 2,000 years ago, where the heat could be as penetrating and overwhelming as the bloated feeling you get after eating a colossal meal. Long before electricity made it possible to make things cold on hot days, humans did their utmost to successfully "store the winter" so it could be used in the summer. In the AD 60s, Emperor Nero served his guests a mixture of crushed fruit and snow with honey in what is considered one of the first recorded examples of sorbet. Snow or ice was stored in caves in the mountains, insulated as well as possible, and then transported to the cities. At first, ice was only for the very richest, but, like spices, it eventually became more widely available to the upper class.

The first predecessors of ice *cream* simply consisted of ice shavings mixed with syrup. This primitive—in the best sense of the word—sorbet or granita is still available in its traditional form in some parts of southern Italy and Sicily. The first time I tried it was in Palermo, where it is sold from little stalls—basically carts with huge blocks of ice on them—where each serving is made individually by scraping the ice to make a portion of snow and then adding whatever flavor you want. It's a concept that lives on in fast-food variants such as Tropical Shave Ice and Tropical Sno. The flavors are often hyper-synthetic—no fruit is ever harmed during the production of this luminescent blue raspberry syrup—but the technique remains almost unchanged.

WHEN THE ROMAN Empire collapsed, all the knowledge about making ice cream vanished. People could no longer afford something so—regardless of how wonderful it was—unnecessary. But the tradition continued in the most prosperous cultures, like China, the courts of Persia, among the Mughal emperors of India, and the Arab nobility. As long as there was money, there was almost no limit to how much of it people were willing to spend on the pleasure of having something cold when everything else was hot. The most extravagant example of this comes from the court of Akbar the Great in Agra, India, in the 1500s, where scientists found that water could be cooled by mixing it with saltpeter—the expensive chemical used in explosives and ammunition. It was, in other words, an extraordinarily resource-consuming way of making a cold bath to put your juice or wine in. A few decades later this research work continued in Naples. "I will show how wine may freeze in glasses," wrote Giambattista della Porta, the polymath who often referred to himself as "professor of secrets" in his book *Magia naturalis* (Natural Magic). Della Porta himself claimed that he was the original inventor of the telescope, but was cheated of the honor by Galileo Galilei; more or less the same thing allegedly happened with several other things he worked on, such as a distillation apparatus and variants of camera obscura. But he remains unquestionably the inventor of something equally important to humanity, namely the basis of ice cream. "The chief thing desired at feasts is that wine, cold as ice, may be drunk, especially in summer," writes della Porta, who offered a recipe not only for chilled wine, but for wine so frozen it was the equivalent of a wine-based popsicle. But this was long before people cared about what children enjoyed. "Put wine into a vial, and put a little water to it, that it may turn to ice the sooner. Then cast snow into a wooden vessel, and strew into it saltpeter powdered . . . Turn the vial in the snow and it will congeal by degrees." By combining ice or snow with saltpeter's ability to lower the temperature, it was possible to achieve temperatures well below freezing.

Saltpeter was still very expensive, although luckily it was soon discovered that you could achieve almost the same effect by combining quite ordinary salt with snow or ice, and it was this principle that was used until modern electric refrigeration was introduced in the 1900s. At my country house I have a hand-cranked ice cream machine that works according to the same principle; a watertight metal flask full of ice-cream mix that you immerse in a mixture of salt and ice and then crank until the contents have turned to ice cream. I've measured the temperature of the ice and salt bath and found it to be 14°F (−10°C).

IF YOU'VE NEVER tasted a real Italian lemon sorbet, then you have one of life's small wonders to look forward to. Nothing tastes so lemony. Nothing is as cold. While many modern restaurants use ice cream machines that give it a velvety soft consistency, the Italian *sorbetto* should be a little more granular, not an imperfection but a deliberate attempt to maintain its likeness to the more crystalline *granita*, the snow that Nero served, and to the home-cranked version. It stings your tongue and palate a little, like eating a handful of snow when you're out skiing.

Lemon sorbet provides a shot of energy, enough to wake up your entire body, even when you've eaten too much. Within all the cold, sharp sourness you can also detect the unmistakable taste of something sweet. Your blood sugar rises and you're lifted from the crippling fullness you might be experiencing.

Today it's hard to imagine a world without sugar. It's as impossible as picturing what your family would have been like if your grandmother had never been born. Sugar has become an elemental flavor, not only in desserts but in most foods, in life itself even, a part of the DNA of our existence. Starting from the dawn of time, before we were humans, we began developing a taste-instrument that could recognize and value sugar. When food tasted sweet—whether it was honey, berries, or fruit—it was a sign that it contained readily available calories, a rare shortcut to nutrition in a world full of bitter-tasting roots. Sugar was first considered a spice, an exclusive commodity with origins in the Buddha's home district, Gur, in what is now Bengal. It was a curiosity, "a reed that gives honey without the aid of bees," as Toussaint-Samat quotes from a 2,500-year-old Persian source. Along with pepper and other spices, sugar found its way to Europe as yet another luxury for the rich and powerful.

Like lemons, sugar cane was brought to Europe by Arabs during the Middle Ages. And as with lemons, it was difficult to find a suitable place to grow the sun-loving and labor-intensive tubes. Some fairly successful sugar plantations were established on the island of Crete, which for a long time went by the name of Candia—a word that basically means "crystallized sugar"—but there were few suitable places in Europe where it could be grown otherwise. Sugar was eventually grown on the European-controlled Canary Islands and Madeira, but not in large enough quantities for it to be widely known. Sweet tastes—depending on how strong they were—were satisfied by honey or different fruit juices.

However, the European conquest of America changed this. At first the continent had been a bit of a disappointment. There were riches to plunder, of course, but America wasn't India, chili and allspice were not pepper, and El Dorado was a myth. The natives—those who hadn't died from the diseases brought by the

Europeans—proved reluctant to cooperate. Sure, they had found what they considered to be a brand new continent, but it was hard to know what to do with it. Until they discovered that several regions—especially the Caribbean islands and the coast leading to what is today Brazil—were particularly suitable for cultivating sugar cane.

When sugar from the New World came on the market, rather than satisfying our hunger, it instead aroused an even deeper one. There are no precise figures on sugar consumption in the late Middle Ages before the discovery of America; it was probably just a few spoonfuls per person per year, mostly honey, and mostly consumed by a tiny elite. But an ever-increasing supply led to a sugar rush. By the year 1700, the average consumption of sugar had reached several pounds a year, and it only continued to grow.

THE SUGAR PLANTATIONS of Brazil and the Caribbean were manned by slaves in order to meet Europe's seemingly insatiable demand. Of the approximately 12 million slaves that were brought across the Atlantic, about 90 percent were sent to sugar-producing areas. The consumption of manpower was enormous, as was the competition between the various slaveholding nations. "If it was to be profitable, such an industry could not afford to pay wages," writes Toussaint-Samat. Sweetness came at a high price.

And when slavery was finally over, after centuries of suffering, Europeans found ways of making their own sugar. The introduction of sugar beet—a sugary relative of beetroot that could also be grown in temperate parts of Europe—pushed down sugar prices, which left those growing it unable to get out of poverty.

By the 1900s, sugar had become so cheap that it began appearing virtually everywhere; not just in snacks, drinks, and desserts, but in savory food as well. Our innate craving for sweet tastes—stemming from the time a ripe fruit or a honeycomb plundered from angry bees was a key to our survival—had led us into addiction. The average American consumes over 7 ounces (200 g) of sugar a day, 175 pounds (80 kg) a year. The tiny leap in blood sugar I'm now feeling, with my spoon dug deep into my lemon sorbet, is the high that unites people of all nations and religions.

WHAT WE EAT has changed who we are, both physically and mentally. Food is history's secret driving force. It has given us strength and energy, and stimulated our collective curiosity, since the very first meal we grilled over the fire. Eating is one of the most universal things we humans do; it binds us together. At the same time, it is also intimate and private, a world no one else can access. I can smell a lamb casserole and be transported to my grandmother's kitchen while feeling a sense of longing and closeness. Or I might feel suddenly disgusted when tasting something, without fully understanding why, before realizing that I last ate it when I was sick or heartbroken.

The same goes for the intense taste of lemon in the sorbet. It not only stings my palate, but my heart as well.

A few years ago in South Africa I planted a garden, on an orchard and vineyard one hour from Cape Town. For the most part, it was an absurdly ambitious project. We had over 120 different types of tomatoes, a variety of salads and herbs, more than fifty different types of peach and nectarine. Not least, we had a citrus grove consisting of all sorts of different lemons, clementines, and oranges. For several months we'd driven around collecting trees from commercial farms throughout the Western Cape. We'd also bought experimental varieties from the Citrus Research Center in Port Elisabeth 430 miles (690 km) away, which required our own permits and a not exactly simple logistical operation. It was a long way from being a success. The oranges were so-so, perhaps because it was too cold, maybe too hot, or most likely not hot or cold enough at the right time. The pomegranates remained small and sour. And in the herb garden there was constant war between the varieties of fast-growing mint and everything else, a war that was difficult to prevent the mint from winning. Yet the triumphs were more important than the defeats. I had never been quite this close to food, and I would go round each day with a basket and pick a random selection of tomatoes; some were small, some large, some red, while others were striped, yellow, brownish, or even white. I made more or less the same tomato salad every day. And every day it tasted different. Each mouthful had its own flavor nuances, and each tomato tasted more like tomato than anything I'd tasted before.

The same went for the lemons. They were just extraordinary. Some were small and almost perfectly round, full of juice that tasted so mild and pleasant it was as if someone had sung to them and smoothed away their defiant bitterness. Others were as big as small melons, and so acidic it was impossible not to grimace when you tasted them, but at the same time impossible to resist. Just one more taste. Ouch! Delicious! Ouch! Yet others had a clean, acidy sharpness, as if you could taste the knife they were sliced with. The most weird and wonderful—if not the best—were the Buddha's hand lemons. Some of these were like clenched fists with deep furrows running the length of the oblong fruit. The most spectacular were splayed like a dozen fingers, and actually looked more like an octopus than a hand, but they smelled more lemony than any other lemon I've come across. I loved walking through the garden, smelling the lemon blossom, taking the Buddha by the hand to release its aroma from the peel, and picking a little fruit from each tree. The juice from the different lemons was made into lemonade, sorbet, or granita.

It was an attempt to create a kind of Garden of Eden, full of different flavors. But for various reasons it couldn't last. The garden required a lot of work, so it could easily have been a full-time job. And the chances of creating an income when you have a little bit of everything, but not much of anything, are microscopic. There was some demand. If I took a box of fruit and vegetables into town when I was going to eat at a restaurant, I would often get dinner and a message from the chef saying he would like regular deliveries. But I never found myself spending hours each day delivering lemons and tomatoes, and we found no other way to make it all profitable, or even cover the expenses. We gradually dropped the vegetables, and a few years later we uprooted the peach and nectarine trees. I still sometimes find myself caressing a lemon I've bought, if it's a particularly beautiful one, or one with tiny dots and lumps that make me think of it as more natural, in which case I always hope that it will taste like one of the lemons from the garden. But I'm nearly always disappointed. Ordinary lemons taste like a shadow of how I know they can taste; like vinegar in yellow packaging.

But in a genuine *sorbetto di limone*, made with lemons from Amalfi, the lemon tastes just like the lemons from the garden. When the sorbet is made properly—with lemons that have ripened on the branch, using some of the aromas from the peel or even the blossom—it is *then* the full taste of lemon. In South Africa I was proud that my lemons and tomatoes were *as good as those in Italy*. Now I'm sitting here, in Italy, enjoying the wonderful, ice-cold sting of my lemon sorbet. And I close my eyes and imagine that I'm in the garden, enjoying the taste of something that is not entirely lost, while I can remember it.

A RESTAURANT IS a closed world. We, the guests, are totally incapacitated. Sure, we can choose; sometimes there are even pages and pages of options. But we have no influence over how the food is prepared or how it will taste. Or what the food will do to us. Eating at a quality restaurant is like being caressed. It gives you a sense of contentment—like I have now—a comfort that goes deep into your body and soul. As I sit here slurping the last partly melted drops of sweet and sour lemon, I feel something reminiscent of happiness.

I pay the bill and walk out into the Roman night. Campo de' Fiori is full of people who are gathered around the fountain and the statue of Giordano Bruno; the bars seem to be almost bleeding people into the square. The apartment I'm staying at is just a few yards away, but instead of going home I decide to walk around the city, down Via Giulia, where I can peer into the elegant courtyards with their pots of ornamental lemons competing with the smell of the city. I also pass Assunta Madre, the fashionable seafood restaurant that was closed down the previous year. Police suspected that Assunta Madre, like many other places in the city, was owned by the Mafia, and as a result the owner, Gianni Micalusi, and his sons were given several years' jail time for money laundering and cooperating with the Mafia. Nevertheless, it hasn't stopped the restaurant—where photos of Gianni posing with celebrities like Robert de Niro, Elton John, and Giorgio Armani adorn the walls—from being fully active again.

In the late 1980s and early 1990s, there were signs that the authorities were finally getting rid of the Mafia. A group of investigating magistrates, led by Giovanni Falcone and Paolo Borsellino, had been given broad powers, which led to several Mafia leaders being imprisoned and convicted. In January 1992, 338 mafiosi, nineteen of whom were Mafia leaders, were sentenced to a total of 2,665 years in prison. The verdict not only represented the conclusion of what is referred to as "the world's largest trial," but was the first time the existence of the Mafia—*Cosa Nostra*—was recognized by the legal system. Until then it had been normal to deny it existed at all. But the Mafia's reprisals demonstrated that the organization was alive and well and that it wasn't going to be stopped by suit-wearing Mafia hunters. Shortly after the trial, in May 1992, Giovanni Falcone was assassinated. His closest associate, Paolo Borsellino, went to Rome to report to the Interior Ministry, suspecting that high-ranking officials and politicians were part of a network that not only was opposed to what he and Falcone were doing, but was directly or indirectly responsible for his partner's death. Whenever he was in Rome, Borsellino had dinner at La Carbonara. "They had actually planned to kill him here, while he was eating," the owner, Dario, once told me while we were talking. "But they decided not to. Rome is far too confusing, especially right here. It's too hard to escape. Too many alleys. Too many people." Two days later, Borsellino was killed by a car bomb outside his mother's house on the outskirts of Palermo. What was to be "the final battle against the Mafia" instead ended with Silvio Berlusconi being elected prime minister in 1994—ensuring what has often been considered a new period of cooperation between the underworld and those at the top. How things stand today, I honestly don't know. There is constant debate about whether the Mafia situation is slightly worse or slightly better than when Falcone and Borsellino began their work.

I WALK PAST Vicolo del Malpasso, where Valentina's restaurant Il Drappo used to be, now occupied by a modern Michelin-starred restaurant that serves food resembling spheres. I cross Corso Vittorio Emanuele II and Piazza dell'Orologio, then enter the narrow side street Vicolo dell'Avila with its restaurants and bars, weaving my way through the city, down streets and up alleyways, walking off the heavy meal. Tomorrow I'll get up, pack my bags, and go home, to my real home, to everyone I miss, but also to the normality of a place that isn't Rome.

It's an aimless walk; I'm not going anywhere. But my body clearly knows where it's going. Eventually I turn onto Via dei Coronari, and I then understand what's happened. It was the sorbet. Because suddenly I'm standing there, outside Gelateria del Teatro, and I'm overjoyed to see that they're not yet closed. One of the employees wipes the benches down for the evening while the last customers stand indecisively in front of the counter, overwhelmed by the selection. Lavender and ricotta, rosemary and honey—a hundred different flavors, probably. Choosing is almost impossible, even if you have conservative taste. If you want chocolate, you have to choose between chocolate fondant, chocolate sorbet, chocolate with Peruvian or Malagasy cocoa, stracciatella, and white chocolate with basil. It's the closest you can get to ice-cream art. Even the combinations that sound weird or bad, such as red wine and chocolate, raspberries and sage, or jam and salt mascarpone, are small revelations. But there's a time for everything. One for trying something new, and one for enjoying something familiar. I buy myself another scoop of *sorbetto di limone*, and let the bittersweet taste of lemon and longing follow me into the night.

SOURCES

The Oxford Companion to Food by Alan Davidson (3rd edn, Oxford, 2014) is without doubt the most important reference book about food. The subject of food is often surrounded by myth and approximation—and Davidson is generous enough to retell good stories and gossip—but he never lets it get in the way of what is a thorough, fact-based review of everything from Aardvark to Zucchini. He is one of the writers who presents the alternative story about the origins of carbonara: that it might have been a result of the generous rations and conservative tastes of American soldiers during the occupation of Italy after the Second World War. If I ever wonder about something, or I'm dealing with conflicting information, this is the book I turn to: readable, entertaining, and authoritative. It is also available in a budget edition with exactly the same text, called *The Penguin Companion to Food*.

Empires of Food by Evan D. G. Fraser and Andrew Rimas (Berkeley, CA, 2012) deals with the various "food empires" that have been the basis for human activity and expansion. It contains a number of interesting historical reviews, one of which was a source for the story about how a dependency on wheat was crucial to the development of the Roman Empire. A recurring theme for the authors is how food empires, like other empires, grow, then collapse. They see parallels between previous food empires and our own, which they believe are threatened by overpopulation, intensive farming techniques, and global warming.

Fraser and Rimas's first book together, *Beef*, with the subtitle *The Untold Story of How Milk, Meat, and Muscle Shaped the World* (New York, 2008), has also been useful to me, especially the chapter concerning meat in general. The book is about man's relationship to cows: how we tamed them, how they have been used for food and as an invaluable work animal, and how modern agriculture has transformed the animal further as a result of today's industrial farming.

A Culinary History of Food is an anthology with a variety of contributors that offers a European, and above all Italian and French, look at the last 2,000 years of food history, edited by Jean-Louis Flandrin and Massimo Montanari (New York, 1999). The parts about early history and Rome's classical period have been particularly useful, and of these articles I would especially like to highlight "The Grammar of Roman Cooking" by Florence Dupont. One of the book's editors, the French historian Flandrin, is also the man behind the hypothesis that the pope's relationship with butter during Lent contributed to the Reformation, and that the border between Catholic and Protestant countries largely corresponds to the border between oil eaters and butter eaters, respectively. The hypothesis is mentioned in his book *Arranging the Meal: A History of Table Service in France* (Berkeley, CA, 2007), and from what I can determine, it was first explained in the article "Le Goût et la nécessité: sur l'usage des graisses dans les cuisines d'Europe occidentale," published in the second issue of the journal *Annales* in 1983. It may be worth noting that the obvious exception to this rule—France—has also been discussed in detail. France already had a kind of butter uprising a few decades before

Luther, which had ended up with the hearty eater Anne of Brittany negotiating for the absolution of large sections of the population in order for them to eat butter on fasting days, when she married France's king in 1491.

Stewart Lee Allen takes a wry look at food in his highly informative and just-speculative-enough book *In the Devil's Garden* (New York, 2003). Allen takes the seven deadly sins as his starting point and explores Rome's excesses, famines, and religious wars. I found his portrayal of the battle over Communion bread particularly enjoyable. In his book about coffee, *The Devil's Cup: A History of the World According to Coffee* (New York, 1999), Allen tries to show how the advent of coffee laid the foundation for the enlightened Western culture that emerged in coffeehouses of London and Paris in the eighteenth century.

An Edible History of Humanity (New York, 2008) by Tom Standage is in my opinion one of the most well-crafted popular-science books about the history of food, and not least about the role of food as a driving force throughout history. This is a really fun and well-written book that follows the story of what Standage describes as "the edible foundations of civilization"—from the introduction of agriculture, through food's role in the establishment of social structures, trade, industrialization, war, and population growth. Standage is currently a member of the editorial board at *The Economist*, and has an economist's view of world development: a liberal with a kind of non-Marxist version of a materialist worldview.

Standage is also the author of another book that's worth reading, about how different drinks have affected world history, *A History of the World in 6 Glasses* (New York, 2005), where he divides world history into different phases based on the dominant drinks of each phase. Beer is the first on his list, possibly invented accidentally when some grain fermented by itself; then wine, during antiquity; spirits, as an important beverage during the transatlantic slave trade; coffee, during the Enlightenment; and tea, during the age of imperialism; while we now live in the age of global American capitalism—the Coca-Cola age.

One of my sources of inspiration as a food writer has for a long time been Jeffrey Steingarten, *Vogue*'s long-time food writer, who in addition to having a remarkable job as a writer for people who don't eat is also one of the most knowledgeable and funny writers I know of, not to mention a good friend. It was Jeffrey who arranged the salt-tasting workshop that I write about in the chapter on salt, and his article about the tasting is reproduced in the collection *It Must've Been Something I Ate* (New York, 2002), in which I make a brief appearance in one of the other articles. His book *The Man Who Ate Everything* (New York, 1998) is a classic that I encourage all food and information junkies to read—among other things, it includes an interesting discussion about the origins of pasta, which I use in the chapter on pasta.

Food in History by Reay Tannahill (New York, 1988), originally published in 1973, claims to be the first book to follow the complete history of food, from our pre-human origins to modern times. It is a broadly told story, which, conscious of its being the first, attempts to be encyclopedic, and so is perhaps best read as such, in small portions at a time. I've enjoyed reading the sections on bread and the domestication of animals, and would particularly like to highlight the story about the very first humans, which I recount in the chapter about fire, even though I make it clear that I disagree almost entirely with this portrayal.

A History of Food by Maguelonne Toussaint-Samat (Oxford, 1992; originally published in French as *Histoire naturelle et morale de nourriture* in 1987) is an eight-hundred-page book about virtually everything that can be eaten and, apart from Davidson's book, has been my favorite reference work for the past twenty years. It is a book that can be read both chronologically and as a reference work; as a great story about man's relationship to food throughout our civilization and history; and, as I have done mostly, as a source for various individual topics such as the cultivation of olives or the spice trade. As befits any French book, a recurring theme is how different foods eventually made it onto French tables, inspired French artists, found their place in a French landscape—so you are never in any doubt about where the center of the universe is in this book.

Italian food

Delizia! by John Dickie (London, 2008) is a sometimes hysterically funny book about Italian food and the Italians' relationship with it. One of the book's main claims is that Italian food was a creation of the city, despite the fact that Italians themselves insist that nearly all their dishes have roots in the countryside. Dickie also has an exciting story about the origins of pasta, about Renaissance food, and why the first pizza to see the light of day was disgusting. Dickie is otherwise best known for his books about Cosa Nostra and the Mafia, which are also highly readable. In *Cosa Nostra* (London, 2004), he also gives an account of the connection between the emergence of the Mafia and the lemon export trade, which I have reproduced myself in the chapter about lemon.

The Food of Italy by Waverly Root (New York, 1971) is a well-written, perhaps slightly outdated introduction to Italian food. Root was a journalist and long-time European correspondent for several American newspapers—and a food lover. He was one of the first to examine the story of food and make it an equally important part of a country's description as its sculptures, paintings, and politics. His breakthrough as a food historian came in 1958 with *The Food of France*. In *The Food of Italy* he looks at the Italian regions and their cuisine; and shows how different waves of invasions affected Italian food, so much so that you can still taste the influence of the Etruscans and Saracens. The book is funny and wise, although I personally think that he puts slightly too little emphasis on how food influenced history.

How Italian Food Conquered the World by John F. Mariani (New York, 2011) is an interesting book about the creation of Italian food, which focuses particularly on the way Italian American immigrants shaped the global understanding of Italian food.

Individual ingredients, cooking, and foodstuffs

Six Thousand Years of Bread: Its Holy and Unholy History by H. E. Jacob (Garden City, NJ, 1944) is one of the earliest food histories and follows the history of bread from its origins in the Levant. Jacob, who came from a prominent Jewish family in Berlin, was sent to the concentration camps at Dachau and Buchenwald. After his family managed to free him from Buchenwald in 1939, he fled to the

United States. Jacob's account of how he and his fellow prisoners made bread from sawdust has no direct relevance to the story told in my book, it's nevertheless worth noting since it gives the food story an extra unpleasant and thought-provoking dimension.

Elaine Khosrova's book *Butter: A Rich History* (Chapel Hill, NC, 2016) is an inspiring book about the cultural and general history of butter, as well as its use in the kitchen. It came in useful for the chapter on oil, where its relationship to butter is repeated.

Salt: A World History by Mark Kurlansky (New York, 2002) is the story of humankind's lasting dependency on salt. Kurlansky has become a leading exponent of a form of microhistory, where he looks at the world from an unusual perspective and often focuses on a specific food. His breakthrough as a writer came with a book about cod, and he has written subsequent books about oysters and milk, among other things.

Spices have long fascinated me, and in my book *Where Flavor Was Born: Recipes and Culinary Travels along the Indian Ocean Spice Route* (San Francisco, CA, 2007), I attempted to embark on a culinary journey while examining the history of spices. The chapter on spices is partly based on this work.

When it comes to books about alcohol, few beat *A Short History of Drunkenness* by Mark Forsyth (London, 2017). The book has a meandering style, as if it was written at the golden point of the evening, somewhere around the third glass, and sometimes professes to be a defense of drunkenness rather than a history book. But despite the informal style, the book, through extensive use of sources, argues in general that alcohol has been present throughout history, and has been hugely important to both our well-being and civilization.

Drink: A Cultural History of Alcohol by Iain Gately (New York, 2009) is a more sober presentation of alcohol's history, but Gately, like Forsyth, also tries to show that fermented, alcoholic drinks are more than just something people enjoy in their spare time; they are "a fundamental part of western culture."

When I was studying at the University of Oslo, the historian Bjørn Qviller was an ever-present factor in the pub, where he would entertain interested students with anecdotes, primarily ones that were about alcohol. When I later had him as a lecturer, the theme was much the same, and a few years later he presented his major work *Battles and Bottles* (Oslo, 2004). While drinking has often been condemned as an unnecessary indulgence, Qviller shows how it was a central part of life in classical Greece.

In *Inventing Wine* (New York, 2012), literature professor Paul Lukacs offers an insight into 8,000 years of wine history and the many changes that have taken place in this time. For me, the book has been specifically useful for its presentation of how wine originated and how it was used during antiquity.

Dangerous Tastes: The Story of Spices by Andrew Dalby (Berkeley, CA, 2000) is, as the title says, the story of spices. The book was a useful overview of this topic and provided me with a lot of histor-ical background, as well as funny anecdotes and reproductions of early historical sources.

The Scents of Eden: A History of the Spice Trade by Charles Corn (New York, 1998) is based on the trade from the "Spice Islands" or the Moluccas in what is today Indonesia. Corn is also particularly interested in Salem, Massachusetts, which played an important role during America's formative years. The parts where Corn tells the more general story of spice were the most useful.

For the past ten years, Reaktion Books has published the exciting Edible series of books, each of which addresses a range of different themes and micro-themes within food and drink, all with the subtitle *A Global History*. In some cases—with spices, potatoes, herring, and olives for example—it's possible to say that the food has been of huge global significance. In other cases—such as cocktails, melons, caviar, or sandwiches—it's perhaps a little harder to spot. These delightful books provide brief overviews of each food's history, initially taking a global perspective that often narrows down to focus mostly on the contemporary USA or Great Britain. I particularly enjoyed reading the books *Beef* (by Lorna Piatti-Farnell, London, 2013), *Lamb* (Brian Yarvin, 2015), *Ice Cream* (Laura Weiss, 2011), and *Lemon* (Toby Sommerman, 2012).

Classic texts

De re coquinaria or *De re culinaria* is one of the world's first cookbooks, written sometime during the first century AD. It is usually referred to as the work of Marcus Gavius Apicius, and commonly referred to as Apicius, although it's somewhat doubtful whether he actually wrote the ten manuscripts of roughly outlined recipes. These recipes are not always very useful, because, as it is stated in Project Gutenberg's translation of the work: "Most of the Apician directions are vague, hastily jotted down, carelessly edited." Never-theless, the text offers a unique insight into the cuisine of the upper-class Romans who lived 2,000 years ago—with a few memor-able culinary quirks: "Scald and wash the flamingo," begins one recipe that concludes by saying that parrot can be cooked in the same manner.

It is available in various translations, including for free online: www.gutenberg.org and http://penelope.uchicago.edu; and Apicius, *Cookery and Dining in Imperial Rome*, ed. Joseph Dommers Vehling (New York, 1977).

A *Voyage Home to Gaul* is a translation of a text by Rutilius Namatianus, a statesman, poet, and historian from Gaul who lived in the fifth century in the final days of the Roman Empire. His text *De reditu suo* is a travelogue from Gaul, which includes a nice description of salt production. The book was published in English as part of the Loeb Classical Library, and is now available without copyright restrictions at http://penelope.uchicago.edu.

The Aeneid by Virgil is the national poem of the Roman Empire. As a historical work, it is both dubious and central: dubious because it barely contains any factual information about Rome's origins, central because the myths on which it is based have helped shape Rome's understanding of itself. The work is available in a number of translations, including Sarah Ruden's modern translation into English (New Haven, CT, 2009).

The Persian poet, scientist, and polymath Omar Khayyam is almost certainly credited with more poems than he actually wrote. A common theme in many of them is the joy of drinking wine, and the irritation at those who want to limit drinking. *Rubaiyat of Omar Khayyam* (London, 1989).

Other books

The biologist Jared Diamond has a tendency to cause controversy with his catchy mega-theories. Although it's important to take some of his explanations with a pinch of salt, it's almost impossible to escape his books when writing about human history, especially when, as with this book, you are trying to find some broad and long brushstrokes. In *Guns, Germs, and Steel: The Fates of Human Societies* (New York, 2007) he addresses Eurasian hegemony—why people from one part of the world have dominated in so many fields. He denies this having anything to do with racial superiority. Instead, he points to nature and the environment, and his argument is full of handy overviews about the origins of agriculture and how farm animals became domesticated, something I use in the chapters on bread and meat. The books *Collapse* and *The World until Yesterday* also focus on food production. In an article in *Discover* magazine from 1999, he claims that the introduction of agriculture was "the worst mistake in human history."

When *Catching Fire* by Richard Wrangham (New York, 2009) first came out, it drew a lot of attention. Wrangham, a professor of biological anthropology at Harvard, presented an entirely new way of looking at human evolution: instead of humans becoming so smart that they were able to control fire, he turned the causation on its head. The fact that our early ancestors learned to control fire enabled them to heat food, which was a prerequisite for the development of today's modern humans and their large brains. It is this portrayal that I use in the chapter about meat. Wrangham's hypothesis about "the Cooking Ape" is still controversial, but—as ever new discoveries of controlled fire dating further and further back in time are made—acceptance of it has grown.

Against the Grain: A Deep History of the Earliest States by James Scott (New Haven, CT, 2017) is a round-up of the last 12,000 years of human history. Why did we give up our lives as hunter-gatherers in favor of agriculture? While this has previously been seen as a step forward, Yale professor Scott argues that it has brought less freedom and a number of disadvantages.

Sapiens by Yuval Noah Harari (New York, 2015) is a well-written and exciting review of the human transition from hunter-gatherers to farmers. In addition to this, Harari offers provocative and startling answers to why we have organized our societies as we have done, and how our imagination and appetite for gossip has helped further human society.

SPQR by Mary Beard (London, 2015) is one of many good history books about Rome. It is the book I have relied on most in terms of historical background information, and a general millennial account of the history of Rome and the Roman Empire. Funny and well written.

In *The Beginnings of Rome: Italy and Rome from the Bronze Age to the Punic Wars* (London, 1995), historian Tim Cornell traces the story of Rome, from its origins as a small Iron Age village to being a major power in the Mediterranean.

Rome: New Fascists, Red Terrorists and the Dream of La Dolce Vita by Simen Ekern (Oslo, 2011) is an exciting introduction to parts of Rome's recent history and culture. It takes us to places that are otherwise difficult to discover, and offers important local insights you wouldn't otherwise find.

Mafia: Inside the Dark Heart by A.G.D. Maran (London, 2008) is the exciting and disheartening story of the Italian Mafia. For me, the most startling and relevant thing about this story was how the Mafia's growth was linked to the lemon trade, and how the Mafia hunters Falcone and Borsellino operated.

The Rise of Rome by Anthony Everitt (New York, 2012) concerns Rome's early history and is divided into three parts: "Legend," dealing with the first part of the city's history, which relies heavily on slightly fanciful stories like the one about the city's founders Romulus and Remus; "Story," which deals with the emergence of a formal state, where myths and historical facts live side by side and are hard to distinguish from one another; and "History," about the republic, where you are presented with a lot of different historical sources. I make good use of his portrayal of historical events and chronology, and it is from Everitt that I have taken the Titus Livius quote.

The Futurist Cookbook by F. T. Marinetti (London, 2014) is a book I have written about several times; in fact one of my first articles on food was specifically about his radical proposal to ban pasta. I also wrote the foreword to the book's Norwegian edition, and repeat some of the points I made there in this book's chapter on pasta.

The Anarchy: The East India Company, Corporate Violence, and the Pillage of an Empire by William Dalrymple (London, 2019) is an entertaining and at the same time frightening book about the rise of the British East India Company. Dalrymple writes little about food but a lot about the company's intrigues, and this contributes to a rich understanding of what was an important period of upheaval: one that laid the foundations for a world order in which a few small European countries ended up controlling almost the entire world.

In *The Covenant of the Wild: Why Animals Chose Domestication* (New York, 1992), Stephen Budiansky shows how the domestication of animals was not just for the benefit of humans, but was something that animals were complicit in. The book is in part a polemic against certain extreme animal-rights activists, but it is first and foremost a call to rethink the important relationship we have with animals— one that has been beneficial to both parties.

Other textbooks

While working on this book I've also really enjoyed a number of other books that have given me both insightful background information and a broader perspective on certain relevant subjects.

Animals as Domesticates: A World View through History by Juliet Clutton-Brock (East Lansing, MI, 2012) is a well-written textbook about the domestication of animals, which explains how this occurred in several places and in different phases, with the domestication of cows, sheep, and goats concentrated in the area around the Fertile Crescent. Clutton-Brock was a leading zooarcheologist, and her book is based largely on archeological material. In the chapter on meat I have quoted from the book's interesting preface, written by James A. Serpell.

Tending Animals in the Global Village: A Guide to International Veterinary Medicine by David M. Sherman (Hoboken, NJ, 2002) features a useful account of how animals have been attracted to human urine, and how this may have contributed to the domestication of several types of livestock.

In *The Archeology of Salt: Approaching an Invisible Past* (Leiden, 2015), editors Brobin Brigand and Olivier Weller present several of the most important discoveries within salt archeology of the last forty years (partly based on a congress held, appropriately enough, at the Dead Sea in Jordan). I particularly enjoyed the articles "First Salt Making in Europe: A Global Overview from Neolithic Times," by Olivier Weller; "The Salt of Rome: Remarks on the Production, Trade and Consumption in the North-Western Provinces," by Ulrich Stockinger; and not least "A Complex Relationship between Human and Natural Landscape: A Multidisciplinary Approach to the Study of the Roman Saltworks in 'Le Vignole-Interporto' (Maccarese, Fiumicino-Roma)," by Maria Cristina Grossi and others, which is a kind of report from the excavations of the salt fields just outside Rome. The whole book is fairly technical, but provides important, concrete information about early salt production.

Robert P. Multhauf's book *Neptune's Gift: A History of Common Salt* (Baltimore, MD, 1978) is considered one of the first modern histories of salt. Here Multhauf explains salt's role as a commodity and not least several of the different techniques used for extracting it. One of the book's interesting points is the distinction Multhauf sets up between two eras: the era of culinary salt and the era of industrial salt (today salt is probably the most important raw material in the chemical industry). It's a fairly technical book and so perhaps not my top recommendation for those who are slightly above averagely interested in salt, unless this interest is combined with an interest in chemistry and industrial history.

If you are over-averagely interested in the corn supply of ancient Rome, *The Corn Supply of Ancient Rome* by Geoffrey Rickman (Oxford, 1980) is the book for you! A short and occasionally tinder-dry book.

Nutrire L'Impero: Storie di alimentazione da Roma e Pompei (Rome, 2015) is a book that was published in connection with a large exhibition about the Roman Empire's food supply at the Museo dell'Ara Pacis in 2015. It consists of a number of short texts about everything from trade and how the port facilities were organized, to kitchen utensils and bread.

A Companion to Food in the Ancient World, edited by John Wilkins and Robin Nadeau (Chichester, 2015), is a collection of academic texts on various aspects of the food system during antiquity, including topics that may initially seem dry and narrow, like Robert Curtis's surprisingly interesting article "Storage and Transport."

Articles and other minor sources

A quick introduction to Giordano Bruno can be found in the *Stanford Encyclopedia of Philosophy*, which is available online: https:// plato.stanford.edu.

"'A Starving Mob Has No Respect': Urban Markets and Food Riots in the Roman World 100 BC–400 AD" by Paul Erdkamp gives an exciting portrayal of the unrest and insecurity over the food supply during the Roman Empire. The article was originally published in the book *The Transformation of Economic Life under the Roman Empire* (Amsterdam, 2002), now available online: www.academia.edu.

Robert Harris has written a number of historical novels and nonfiction books about Rome. In relation to the change in legislation following the September 11 attacks in 2001, Harris also wrote an interesting article in the *New York Times* about the similarities between the reaction to the pirate attacks on Ostia in the year 68 BC and September 11. Robert Harris, "Pirates of the Mediterranean," *New York Times*, September 30, 2006, at www.nytimes.com.

In the *New York Times* article "Just Grate" (March 30, 2008), Robert Trachtenberg writes about the Italians' relationship to the combination of cheese and seafood, and it's from here that I've taken the quote about how Italians love making rules, but are reluctant to follow them. Available online: www.nytimes.com.

Friends of Roman Ostia is a nonprofit organization in the United States that works with the port of Ostia Antica. Their website contains a wealth of interesting information about this important Roman port. The article "The Historical Salt Works of the Coastal Plain of Rome," about the salt fields and the salt production during antiquity and pre-antiquity, was particularly useful in my chapter about salt: www.ostia-foundation.org.

In his article "The Laziness of the Short-Distance Hunter: The Origins of Agriculture in Western Denmark," *Journal of Anthropological Archeology*, III (1984), pp. 300–324, Peter Rowley-Conwy goes through the nutritional sources of hunter-gatherers in Denmark, and how they waited for a long time before they adopted farming. It's an interesting article, because it helps challenge the idea that farming was an improvement on the previous lifestyle.

The story of the Lykov family, who lived in isolation for decades before finally being found, is based on an article on www.smithsonianmagazine.com by Mike Dash, "For 40 Years This Russian Family Was Cut Off from All Human Contact, Unaware of World War II," January 28, 2013, www.smithsonianmag.com. If you are fascinated by the family's story, which I only briefly summarize, they are also the subject of a longer biography written by the journalist Vasili Peskov: *Lost in the Taiga: One Russian Family's Fifty-Year Struggle for Survival and Religious Freedom in the Siberian Wilderness* (New York, 1994).

The *New York Times* article "Lactose Tolerance in East Africa Points to Recent Evolution" (December 11, 2006) talks about researchers from the University of Maryland who found three new mutations that allow some peoples to remain lactose tolerant, even in adulthood: www.nytimes.com.

The readers' letter in *The Spectator* from 1903 about the Italian salt monopoly in digital form: http://archive.spectator.co.uk.

I've taken some facts concerning the abolition of the Chinese salt monopoly from an article in the *Financial Times*: "China Shakes

Up 2,000 Year Old Salt Monopoly," January 2, 2017, online at www.ft.com.

As far as I've been able to ascertain (with the help of Serventi and Sabban, among others) the myth about Marco Polo bringing pasta to Italy comes from the *Macaroni Journal*, the newsletter of the National Macaroni Manufacturers, VI (1929), online at https://ilovepasta.org.

An interesting and sometimes quite technical article on genetics that also touches on the idea of self-domestication is Adam S. Wilkins, Richard W. Wrangham, and W. Tecumseh Fitch, "The 'Domestication Syndrome' in Mammals: A Unified Explanation Based on Neural Crest Cell Behavior and Genetics," *Genetics*, CXCVII/3 (2014), pp. 3795–808. It also includes a useful analysis of Darwin's theories and the experimental research I mention on the domestication of foxes.

The research on the relationship between the Mafia's origins and the lemon trade was first published in the article "Origins of the Sicilian Mafia: The Market for Lemons," written by Arcangelo Dimico, Alessia Isopi, and Ola Olsson, and also in the *Journal of Economic History* in January 2012. It's rare to find an article on economic history that can also be read as a kind of detective story. The article is available online: www.researchgate.net.

Our World in Data is a collaborative project affiliated with the Oxford Martin Program on Global Development. On their website https://ourworldindata.org they have collected a vast amount of information, statistics, and figures about the environment, consumption, and distribution. It's from here that I took most of the figures I use about meat consumption: https://ourworldindata.org.

On several occasions in the book I touch on subjects that I've previously written about. Some ideas and arguments have been repeated and expanded upon, and I have reused some episodes and anecdotes, some in English, which were published in my Gastronomer column in the *Washington Post*, others in my tribal language, Norwegian. Of particular importance is the article about the Garden of Gethsemane that I wrote for *Dagbladet Magasinet* in 2018, "Hellig olje fra den hellige hage," www.dagbladet.no/magasinet/hellig-olje-fra-den-hellige-hage/69655445, March 29, 2018, and my article on Wonderwerk Cave in Morgenbladet, published in January 2016, "Kjøkken Evolusjon," online: https://morgenbladet.no.

Locations in Rome

There are hundreds—if not thousands—of great places to eat in Rome. A few of them appear in this book, in larger or smaller roles, and they are all near Campo de' Fiori, in Centro Storico.

La Carbonara
Piazza Campo de' Fiori, 23, 00186 Rome
Phone: +39 06 686 4783
www.ristorantelacarbonara.it/en

The meal at La Carbonara forms the framework of this book, and this restaurant—located in the bustling square Campo de' Fiori—has been chosen for several reasons, mostly because it has become my favorite haunt in Rome, somewhere I always stop by for lunch or dinner. It's a fairly typical classic Roman restaurant, of which there are a handful—but not much more than a handful. Like most of them it is frequented by a mix of tourists and Romans—mostly the former in the summer, and mostly the latter in the winter. The menu is also similar to those you find in many other, similar restaurants. The wide range of *antipasti* varies seasonally, from artichokes in early spring to porcini in autumn. If you're not going to have pasta carbonara for *primi*, which is the obvious and most popular choice, you might find it fun to try a relative of carbonara, *pasta alla gricia*. Lamb is the best choice among the *secondi*, and for the brave, offal such as sweetbread or brain can be recommended.

Ristorante La Campana
Vicolo della Campana, 18, 00186 Rome
Phone: +39 06 687 5273
www.ristorantelacampana.com/en

Rome's supposedly oldest restaurant, Ristorante La Campana, is located in a small alley just over half a mile north of La Carbonara. The place celebrated its five-hundredth anniversary in 2019, and is, as it should be, a proud guardian of tradition. It is one of those places where you can get a really good classic *vignarola di verdure*—a stew made with broad beans, peas, and bacon; and also one of the few places that still uses a display cabinet for its cold *antipasti* and seasonal specialties. I love the refined, yet modest, dining room as well as the brusque and formal service that occasionally erupts into unexpected friendliness.

Checchino dal 1887

Via di Monte Testaccio, 30, 00153 Rome

Phone: +39 333 585 5055

www.checchino-dal-1887.com

Checchino dal 1887 has what may well be the most unique location in the city—excavated from the shards of ancient Roman olive-oil pots that form Monte Testaccio. Its menu is heavy on offal, from sweetbread to brain, with the occasional tongue or tail for the squeamish. Try *pajata* if you dare, and feel free to request a visit to the wine cellar where you can see the 2,000-year-old pot shards with your own eyes. From spring until autumn, this restaurant has a lovely outdoor dining area on the sidewalk.

Dal Toscano Restaurant

Via Germanico, 58–60, 00192 Rome

Phone: +39 06 3972 5717

www.ristorantedaltoscano.it

Dal Toscano is a meat lover's paradise, a kind of Tuscan embassy near the Vatican, frequented by a mix of locals, clerics, and tourists. This is the place to go for huge meals that consist of grilled meat, meat that for some strange reason comes mostly from Denmark. The crown jewel on the menu is *fiorentina*—T-bone steak—2½ pounds for two people.

Gelateria del Teatro

Via dei Coronari, 65–66, 00186 Rome

Phone: +39 06 4547 4880

www.gelateriadelteatro.it

Where to find Rome's best ice cream is a constant source of heated debate, but my favorite place is Gelateria del Teatro, which offers a number of unique flavor combinations, such as lavender and white peach; rosemary-honey and lemon; and ricotta, figs, and almonds. Although nothing beats the lemon sorbet.

If you are in the area, I would also recommend the wine bars Cul de Sac and Il Goccetto, which are busy and informal; and Roscioli Salumeria, which has an insane selection of wines (and cured meats), but requires you to book a table in advance. If innovative cocktails are your thing then I can recommend the Jerry Thomas Speakeasy, while the city's best seafood, finest outdoor seating, and stiffest prices can be found at Pierluigi. Fabulous cured meats— including good guanciale—are available at Norcineria Viola, in the middle of Campo de' Fiori.

Campo de' Fiori is said to be the only square in Rome without a church. But that doesn't mean that our Lord has forgotten the place. If you look hard enough, on the opposite side to La Carbonara, in the southeast corner of the square, you can find the entrance to Passetto del Biscione, a beautiful little alley with newly restored ceiling murals featuring cherubs and saints. It was here, in 1796, that a miracle allegedly took place: the painting of the Madonna del Latte—the Nursing Madonna—moved her eyes.

Acknowledgments

While I have taken care to list many of the written sources used while working on this book, it's important for me to stress that the learning and experience gained from eating food, at home and in everyday life, on special occasions and as a central part of traveling large parts of the world, makes up just as crucial a part of the research behind this book. The most important starting point for writing this book has been the more than 50,000 meals I've eaten. So the biggest omission from this list of sources is all the meals, all the knowledge transfer that comes from eating, sharing food with others, cooking food yourself, seeing and experiencing others cooking, growing your own food, and being involved with other parts of food production. Without the experience of eating, no book.

The other part of the background work concerns the reading material that has orientated, disorientated, and inspired me. The main idea for the book is mine: I wanted to tell a bigger story about a specific place and about the whole world. Nevertheless, it's an idea inspired by the others who have combined food history and world history in a similar manner. The factual information and many of the case studies are taken from books I have read, most of which are mentioned in the overview. Interested readers can use this overview to go in-depth where I have merely scratched the surface. I've chosen to distinguish between books that have food as their main theme and those which are basically about other things. I've not used footnotes, something academic readers might find annoying, but I have referred to the source in the text when quoting or relating to reasonings from specific books.

I would like to take this opportunity to thank Anne Luziette, Maria Trancassini, and Dario Martelli at La Carbonara; Paolo Trancassini at La Campana; and Francesco Mariani at Checchino dal 1887. Thanks to Associate Professor Knut Ødegård at the University of Oslo's Department of Archeology, Conservation, and History, who was a consultant for the book and gave me important advice and feedback; Simen Ekern, who has been my friend and Rome guide for many years and who read the manuscript, provided useful input, and prevented embarrassing misunderstandings; Orietta Rossini at the Museo dell'Ara Pacis, for helping me with material I wouldn't have had access to otherwise; Henry Notaker for the inspiration and friendship; Paul Clüver for his friendship in food and farming, Vibeke Viestad, who got me to see Rome with new eyes; and the tireless efforts of Maiken Fotland and her colleagues at Kagge Forlag. The text has improved significantly thanks to you. Any errors you might find are entirely mine.